Spor   ries

VOLLEYBALL
Fundamentals

Joel Dearing
Springfield College

Human Kinetics

Library of Congress Cataloging-in-Publication Data

Human Kinetics Publishers.
   Volleyball fundamentals / Human Kinetics with Joel Dearing.
       p.   cm.
    ISBN 0-7360-4508-2 (Soft cover)
   1. Volleyball.   I. Dearing, Joel.   II. Title.
   GV1015.3 .D43   2003
   796.325--dc21

                           2002015234

ISBN: 0-7360-4508-2

Developmental Editor: Cynthia McEntire; **Assistant Editors:** John Wentworth, Kim Thoren; **Copyeditor:** Barb Field; **Proofreader:** Sarah Wiseman; **Graphic Designer:** Robert Reuther; **Graphic Artist:** Francine Hamerski; **Art and Photo Manager:** Dan Wendt; **Cover Designer:** Keith Blomberg; **Photographer (cover and interior):** Dan Wendt; **Illustrator:** Roberto Sabas; **Printer:** United Graphics

Human Kinetics books are available at special discounts for bulk purchase. Special editions or book excerpts can also be created to specification. For details, contact the Special Sales Manager at Human Kinetics.

Printed in the United States   10 9 8 7 6 5 4 3 2 1

Human Kinetics
Web site: www.HumanKinetics.com

United States: Human Kinetics
P.O. Box 5076
Champaign, IL 61825-5076
800-747-4457
e-mail: humank@hkusa.com

Canada: Human Kinetics
475 Devonshire Road Unit 100
Windsor, ON N8Y 2L5
800-465-7301 (in Canada only)
e-mail: orders@hkcanada.com

Europe: Human Kinetics
107 Bradford Road
Stanningley
Leeds LS28 6AT, United Kingdom
+44 (0) 113 255 5665
e-mail: hk@hkeurope.com

Australia: Human Kinetics
57A Price Avenue
Lower Mitcham, South Australia 5062
08 8277 1555
e-mail: liahka@senet.com.au

New Zealand: Human Kinetics
P.O. Box 105-231, Auckland Central
09-523-3462
e-mail: hkp@ihug.co.nz

Welcome to Sports Fundamentals

The Sports Fundamentals Series uses a learn-by-doing approach to teach those who want to play, not just read. Clear, concise instructions and illustrations make it easy to become more proficient in the game or activity, allowing readers to participate quickly and have more fun.

Between the covers, this book contains rock-solid information, precise directions, and clear photos and illustrations that immerse you in the heart of the sport or activity. Each fundamental chapter is divided into four major sections:

- **You Can Do It!:** Jump right into the activity with a clear explanation of how to perform an essential skill.
- **More to Choose and Use:** Find out more about the skill or learn exciting alternatives.
- **Take It to the Court:** Apply the new skill with a focus on safety and effectiveness.
- **Give It a Go:** Place the new skill within a training program that gets results.

No more sitting on the bench! The Sports Fundamentals Series gets you right into the middle of things. Apply the techniques as they are learned, and have fun.

Contents

Acknowledgments

I'd like to acknowledge my colleagues, Dr. William Considine and Dr. Stephen Coulon, at Springfield College who were supportive of my efforts to complete this book. Special thanks also to my long-time coaching companions, Kevin Lynch, Marcus Jannitto, Lev Milman, Mary Lalor, and Charlie Sullivan, and, of course, the man who brought me into the game of volleyball, my coach, Tom Hay. I'm thankful for the lifetime of encouragement I have received from my parents, David and Doris Dearing, along with the joy I have received as a dad to three very special children, Erin, Kevin, and Ryan.

Finally, I'd like to dedicate this book to my forever-love, my wife Diane. Your love is a "pearl."

Introduction:

Before You Rotate

Learning the fundamentals of volleyball can be great fun. Volleyball is a unique, exciting game that requires solid teamwork and consistent individual execution. Unlike many other team sports, players rotate to different positions on the court, so all players must be prepared to play a variety of roles on the team. At elite levels, players may specialize, but beginners and recreational players should learn the basics of all positions.

Before we rotate to cover the fundamental skills of volleyball, let's discuss some basic features and rules of the game. An understanding of these basic rules will be enough to get you started.

Court and Equipment

The volleyball court is 18 meters from endline to endline and 9 meters from sideline to sideline (figure 1). The centerline below the net divides the court in half. Each team's attack line is three meters from the centerline. A back-row player must jump from behind the attack line to legally contact a ball that is above the height of the net. Players may initiate the serve from anywhere along the endline.

For women's volleyball, the net is 2.24 meters (7 feet, 4 -1/8 inches) high; for men's volleyball, the net is 2.43 meters (7 feet, 11-5/8 inches) high. The net should be strung tightly to avoid any sagging and to allow a ball driven into the net to rebound cleanly instead of dropping straight to the floor (figure 2).

Antennae are connected to the volleyball net just above the sidelines. The volleyball must always pass over the net and between the antennae on a serve and throughout a rally. (*Note:* Under the new pursuit rule [effective fall of 2002], the ball can pass outside

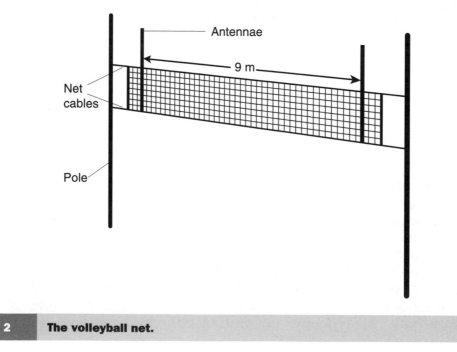

1   The volleyball court.

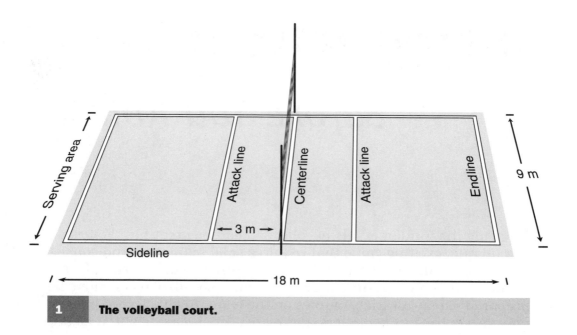

2   The volleyball net.

either antenna on the opponent's side and a player can pursue the ball out of bounds, return it outside the antenna to a teammate, and then send it across the net to the other team.)

What do you need to play? Begin with volleyball shoes, knee pads, and a volleyball. Choose an indoor or outdoor volleyball depending on where you plan to play. Talk to a local volleyball coach for sound advice on what type of ball to purchase.

The proper uniform includes matching T-shirts and shorts, appropriate volleyball shoes, and knee pads (figure 3). If you are starting a new team, you will need to purchase T-shirts numbered on the front and back and then select team shorts. The color and brand should be the same for all players.

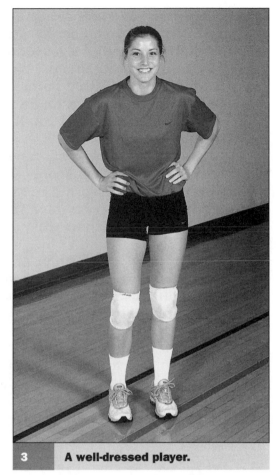

3 A well-dressed player.

Rules

For an indoor, six-person game, each team has six players on the court in a predetermined lineup. Prior to service, players must be in their legal positions to avoid an overlap penalty. An overlap violation will be called if the middle back player is closer to the centerline than the middle front player or if the middle back player is closer to the left sideline than the left back player (see chapter 1 for more about formations). Once the server contacts the ball, players may change positions for the remainder of the rally. Back-row players may play near the net but may not block or attack a ball that is above the height of the net.

A legal serve must cross the net between the antennae. Recent revisions in volleyball rules allow the served ball to contact the net and remain in play. A server who steps on the endline prior to contact is considered in the court, resulting in a serving fault.

The receiving team has three team contacts to return the ball to the other side of the net, but no individual may contact the ball more than once consecutively. An individual or group block does not count as a contact for any player; a player is allowed to block, then make another legal contact with the ball.

Throughout a rally, the ball must cross the net between the antennae. Any ball that lands on a sideline or endline is considered "in." Players may not touch the net. Each time the receiving team wins a rally, the players on that team rotate one position in a clockwise direction.

Rally scoring systems have recently been adopted in volleyball, meaning a point is scored on every play. Rally scoring replaced the traditional scoring method that awarded points only to the serving team. See chapter 13 for more information on scoring systems, including some unique ways to keep track of the score during drills.

In an outdoor beach or grass-court game, players typically play two versus two. The outdoor game provides the additional challenges of playing in the sun and wind. Teams change sides after every 10 points to minimize the advantage of playing on one side of the court over the other. The basic skills (serve, block, set, and attack) are the same for outdoor volleyball.

In contrast to the blocking rule for indoor volleyball, in the beach game, a block does count as an individual and team contact. The outdoor game utilizes the full dimensions of the regulation-size court.

Righties and Lefties

Volleyball terminology includes references to the strong side and weak side. The easiest way to understand these terms is to think about a right-handed player attacking a ball near the left antenna. As it approaches the attacker from a set, the ball arrives at the attacking arm without crossing the player's body. The opposite is true if the right-handed player is attacking the ball near the right antenna. As it approaches the attacker from a set, the ball must go past the body to arrive near the attacking arm.

For right-handed players, the left side of the net is their strong or power side and the right side of the net is their weak side. For lefties, the right side of the net is the strong side and the left side of the net is the weak side. Lefties are referred to as opposites, since they are often placed opposite the setter in the rotation.

Several volleyball skills will be taught without reference to righties or lefties. Footwork patterns associated with serving and attacking will be presented in chapters 3 and 6 with important distinctions suggested for right- and left-handed players.

Left-handed players are often naturals for the setter and opposite positions, since the right side of the net is their power side. Lefties who are excited about taking their game to the next level should attempt to play those positions.

Let's get started with a basic team formation before breaking down into individual skills.

Key to Diagrams

S	Server
T	Target
△	Cone
→	Player movement
---→	Ball movement
⬭	Hula hoop
Ts	Tosser
P	Passer
●	Volleyball
C	Coach/instructor
St	Setter
X	Player
A	Attacker
L	Left-handed player/left side player
R	Right-handed player/right side player
B	Blocker
Sh	Shagger
F	Feeder/female player
D	Digger/defender
⟨8⟩	Left side player
[9]	Designated middle
(10)	Setter/right side player
M	Designated middle/male player

The W Formation

Imagine an activity class playing six on six on the first day of class. It looks just like backyard volleyball. Whether their team is serving or receiving, front-row players typically stand three to five feet away from the net. Back-row players generally stand 15 to 20 feet away from the net in a straight line across the court. Before long, the teams are merely batting the ball back and forth over the net. Occasionally, a gung ho leader emerges on a team, suggesting they get the ball to the middle front person so that player can set or that they use all three legal contacts.

The missing piece of the puzzle is a system of play. The W formation is a good place to start. The W is a basic system that you can begin to use immediately.

Creating the W

If you are like most beginning volleyball players, you probably think of the court as being divided into two zones, front row and back row. Actually, the court has six zones: right back (zone 1), right front (zone 2), middle front (zone 3), left front (zone 4), left back (zone 5), and middle back (zone 6) (figure 1.1).

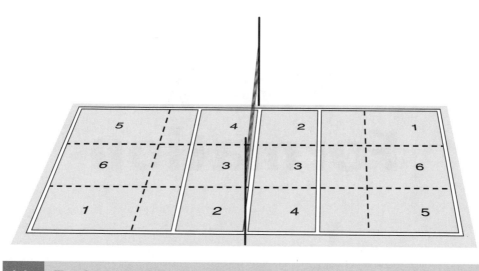

1.1 **The six zones of the volleyball court.**

To create a W formation, the player in zone 2 moves to the net, taking a position to the right of the center of the net. This player is the designated setter, the target for the player who receives the serve. Players in zones 3 and 4 move straight back behind the attack line; they are the primary attackers. The player in zone 1 moves up to form a straight line with the players in zones 3 and 4. The players in zones 5 and 6 position themselves to create the W. All five players are now in position to receive the serve (figure 1.2).

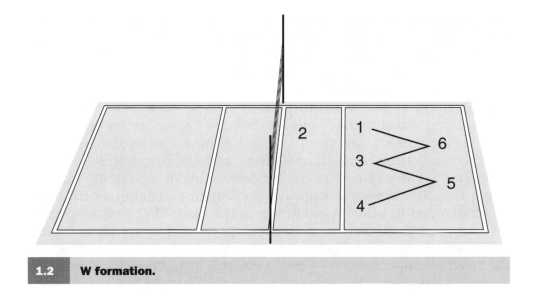

W formation.

Using the W

You can use this basic offensive system immediately to receive serve, even as you are learning how to execute each skill. You also will use this formation during rallies, especially when the opposing team prepares to return the ball across the net without an attack. This is referred to as a *free ball*. Once a team anticipates that their opponents cannot attack their third contact, they simply need to call out "free ball" and move to the W formation. This process is called *transition*. Transition in volleyball will let you play and enjoy the game at a much higher level. (See chapter 11 for more on transition.)

Communication is the key to successful team play. As you learn the fundamentals of volleyball, it is critical to understand the importance of talking as you play. Remember this simple rule: Talk before you contact the ball. You will be playing in a very congested area. The ball moves quickly, and reaction is a big part of the game. As you react to the ball and to each situation, use the communication skills presented throughout this book, such as calling "free ball" when you realize your opponent is not going to attack before sending the ball back over the net.

Keep in mind that if it is important to talk, then somebody must be listening. Presumably, your teammates can count on you to call for the ball consistently. On the other hand, you must also be a good listener and react to the signals given by your teammates.

As you are introduced to the fundamentals of volleyball, you will begin to notice a progression in your learning experience. You will be challenged to understand and practice each skill with emphasis on proper skill execution, to communicate prior to contacts, to follow rules of responsibility that will be established, and to recognize the need to move constantly on the court. The game of volleyball has a flow. Often players become spectators on the court and watch what is happening, rather than staying in the flow.

I remember listening to Doug Beal, the USA Men's National Team coach, talk about how he evaluates players. He likes to watch what players do between contacts. Effective players are active between contacts. They anticipate what might happen next and move on the court in a low position, expecting the ball to come to them.

Two dynamic contacts (serving and attacking) often lead to winning rallies. Topspin is a foundational skill essential in contacting the volleyball with your hand. Let's learn how to do it.

Creating Topspin

Creating topspin is a unique aspect of contacting the volleyball, so it makes sense to get you started with this skill right away. Topspin is needed for effective attacks and topspin serves. Additionally, a player working on defense will need a teacher, coach, or playing partner who can hit with topspin to simulate an attack for the defensive player to dig. Learning how to create topspin at the outset will prove valuable as you move through this text. This skill will be reviewed and implemented throughout.

Making It Spin

Stand six to eight feet away from a wall; you can use a gym, racquet-ball court, or any court space that has a wall. With both hands, hold the volleyball above your head and throw it off the floor with forward spin toward the wall so that the ball rebounds off the floor, hits the wall, and comes back to you (figure 2.1a). Experiment with your throw until you can consistently throw the ball hard enough that it rebounds off the wall with enough force that you need to raise your hands to catch it above your head.

Once you can toss the ball consistently, your next goal will be to attack the rebound with topspin instead of catching it (figure 2.1b). If you are right-handed, stand with your left foot forward. If you are left-handed, stand with your right foot forward. This standing position simulates the position of your body when you jump to attack.

 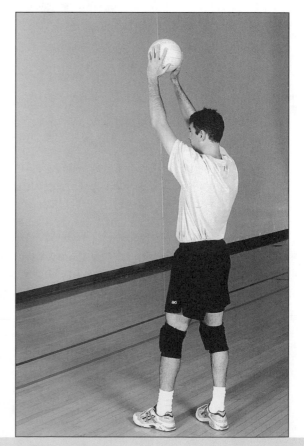

2.1 **a. Throw the ball off the floor.** **b. Add an attack.**

Throw the ball with forward spin off the floor. Open your attacking or serving hand. As the ball rebounds off the wall, reach high with your attacking arm and, keeping your elbow above shoulder height, swing your arm in a whiplike motion (figure 2.1c). Reach and snap your hand forward over the ball. The heel of your hand contacts the ball first. The snapping motion creates topspin.

Stay balanced with your nondominant foot forward. Try to bounce the ball off the floor close to where it hit when you threw it off the floor (figure 2.1d). Practice until you can consistently attack the ball and have it return to you off the wall. Set a goal of throwing the ball off the floor and attacking it with topspin under control three times in a row.

c. Snap your hand over the ball.

d. Bounce the ball off the floor.

Once you have mastered hitting the rebound with topspin, quickly raise both arms after each subsequent attack (figure 2.2) and keep your left foot forward if you are right-handed (if you are left-handed, keep your right foot forward). With both arms raised, you will discover that your nonattacking arm naturally begins to pull down to your side when your attacking hand moves toward the ball.

Making Contact With an Open Hand A common misconception in volleyball is that it's best to attack with a closed fist. The casual ob-

2.2 **Foot forward.**

2.3 **Attack with an open hand.**

server sees an attacker pound the ball and assumes that their fist is supplying the power. This is not true. Attacking the ball with a closed fist is not an effective strategy. Creating topspin with an open hand (figure 2.3) provides more control, causes the ball to drop into the court, and decreases the chances of the ball sailing out of bounds. Work on creating topspin right away!

Tips for Terrific Topspin

As you practice creating top-spin, keep these hints in mind:

- Stay on the balls of your feet and move as needed to adjust to the ball rebounding off the wall.
- Keep the ball in front of you.
- Attempt to contact the ball high and in back of the ball each time.
- Focus on snapping your wrist and creating topspin.
- Remember that the initial throw with forward spin simulates the topspin you will create with your attack.

After you contact the ball, raise both arms and keep your nondominant foot forward in preparation for the next contact.

Give it a go: Topspin

Many volleyball drills require the ball to be tossed. To toss the ball effectively, use both hands, toss from the hip, step with the foot opposite that hip, and try to toss with no spin. Practice with a friend or teammate.

TOSSING PRACTICE

For successful practice, you need to reinforce accurate tossing until it becomes automatic. Split players into groups of two. Partners stand on the attack lines on opposite sides of the net. Partners alternately toss and catch the ball for a total of 20 attempts. Players should toss the ball using two hands (figure 2.4), tossing from the hip with no spin.

2.4   Toss with both hands.

CHAPTER

Serving

Tom Hay, former Springfield College volleyball coach, often reminded his players, "You can't score if you can't serve." You may think this phrase had more meaning before traditional scoring was replaced by rally scoring. However, one could argue that it is even more important now, since a missed serve not only eliminates a chance for your team to score but also gives your opponent a point plus the right to serve.

Although in competitive situations the server does not communicate prior to contact, the coach may signal the server to serve to a specific zone. Serving strategy often targets the opponent's weakest receiver or the gap between two players. Therefore, serving with control is important. Players with booming serves or spectacular jump serves demonstrate that power is also important. Teachers of sport skills often struggle with the debate over power versus control. This chapter emphasizes both. An effective server needs to develop both a powerful serve and the ability to serve to a specific zone.

Overhead Floater

To execute an overhead floater serve, stand comfortably with your nondominant foot slightly forward (figure 3.1a). Be sure that your weight is on your back foot. Hold the ball with your nonserving hand in front of your serving shoulder.

Slide your front foot forward and feel your body weight shift from your back foot to your front foot. As you step forward, toss the ball directly in front of your serving shoulder high enough to force you to reach with your serving hand (figure 3.1b).

The toss requires a lot of attention because many errors result from inconsistent location of the toss. Experienced players commonly use the one-hand toss. The one-hand toss allows you to place your serving arm in a ready or cocked position with your elbow above your shoulder. Keep the height of your toss near the height of your reach. When you toss the ball to this location, you will need to accelerate your hand to the ball. Accelerating your hand to the ball creates power.

3.1 **a. Ready position.**   **b. Toss the ball.**

An effective arm swing has a whiplike action. The arm swing begins as you draw your elbow behind your ear with your attacking hand open and palm facing out (figure 3.1c). Your elbow should remain above the height of your shoulder throughout the whiplike action.

Be sure to reach high and in front of you as you contact the ball. Make contact with an open hand (figure 3.1d). Use a strong hand, keeping your wrist firm throughout contact. Contact the ball with the meaty part of your hand right in the center of the ball. Your fingers should be slightly spread, allowing you to contact more of the surface of the ball.

The floater serve is most effective when follow-through is limited. After accelerating your serving hand to the ball, allow the hand to lower naturally to your side. A long follow-through may generate too much power, causing the serve to travel out of bounds. Limiting the follow-through helps provide the floating movement of the serve as it travels to the opponent. This movement is often compared to a knuckle ball.

c. Draw back the elbow.

d. Make contact.

The sequence of the toss and contact should be rapid. Remember, your hand is accelerating to the ball. As soon as the ball leaves your hand for the toss, the whiplike action or throwing motion of the arm must follow.

There are other ways to put the ball in play than with the over-head floater. The important thing is to use the serve that gives your team the best chance to win a point. Try these variations on the serve and find the one that works best for you and your team.

Stepping Into the Serve   Many players take several steps prior to serving. Keep in mind that you will commit a foot fault if you step on or inside the endline prior to contacting the ball. If you choose to take more than one step before serving, establish a consistent start-ing point behind the endline to avoid foot faults. Generally, taking more than one step does not provide any advantage. The final step forward with the nondominant foot provides enough transfer of weight.

Underhand Serve   The underhand serve (figure 3.2) is a good beginning serve. It does not provide a lot of power, but it can be very accurate and consistent. The rules of volleyball require a toss or release of the ball prior to the serve. Coordination of the toss and contact of an underhand serve is actually quite challenging. Think of the toss in the under-hand serve as a release. Create a pendulum motion with your arms. As the hand holding the ball drops, your serving hand moves forward through the ball. Contacting an underhand serve from a toss can be difficult. Keep the fingers of your serving hand pointing behind your body to ex-pose the heel of your hand to the ball. This will allow you to con-tact the ball with the meaty part of your hand. Many players at-tempt to use a fist for an under-hand serve, but this often causes inconsistent contact. In addition, the open hand leads to a more natural progression from the underhand serve to the over-hand floater.

3.2   **Underhand serve.**

Topspin Serve The primary advantage of developing a topspin serve (figure 3.3) is power. The topspin serve can provide additional power but requires a few changes from the overhead floater serve. One major change is that the topspin serve requires a follow-through. Toss the ball more directly over your serving shoulder. This will force you to step under the ball and snap your wrist with a full follow-through. The snap of the wrist will create topspin (see chapter 2). You may find it helpful to experiment with a slightly higher toss. Remember to accelerate your hand to the ball and keep your elbow above the height of your shoulder throughout the arm swing.

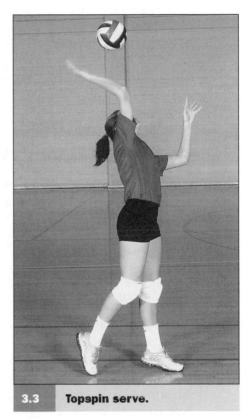

3.3 **Topspin serve.**

3.4 **Jump serve.**

Jump Serve Go for the gold as you bring the heat with your jump serve (figure 3.4). The jump serve can be a tremendous weapon; it is both powerful and deceptive. The jump serve can create apprehension in your opponents if they are not used to facing this type of serve. You may find the jump serve easier after you've mastered attacking (chapter 6). In essence, the jump serve is an attack from the endline. Instead of attacking a set from a teammate, you attack your own toss. Hold the ball in front of your serving shoulder as you prepare for the toss. Use a one-handed toss, but toss the ball with your serving arm. You will launch yourself into the air to attack the toss, so toss the ball high in front of you. It is essential to coordinate the toss with a sequence of steps, allowing you to jump and swing naturally. Step forward on your nondominant foot as you toss the ball.

Serving With Strategy

At the competitive level, serving strategy is based on your philosophy for playing the game. Will you be conservative or assertive? What are the risks and rewards involved in each situation? You need to answer these types of questions when you take it to the court.

Serving strategy often means serving to a particular zone of your opponent's court. Be sure you can identify the zones of the court as you look across the net (see page 2).

Initial serving strategy could include the following objectives:

- Serving to the opponent's weakest receiver
- Serving between two players
- Serving short (near or in front of the opponent's attack line)
- Serving to the deep third of the opponent's court

Notice that the first three involve the need for serving control and the final objective requires serving power.

The team's or coach's philosophy also will affect serving strategy, as does level of play. Highly skilled players can control the ball on offense and attack at a high rate of efficiency. Strong, effective serves are needed to force an opponent into poor ball control, leading to a less successful attack from the opponent. At a lower or intermediate level, effective serving may require a high percentage of serves simply to be in play, since the opponent's offense may not be overpowering.

Here are some additional serving strategies:

- Serve to the opponent's front-row attackers. Challenge the opponent's strongest attacker to pass the ball, then attack.
- Develop a philosophy of serving, taking into consideration those times when it may be critical not to miss a serve—game point, match point, after an opponent's service error, after your team misses a serve, and immediately following a time-out.
- If the setter has to move from her legal court position to the net, serve into the setter's path, causing her to react to the ball while moving. Ideally, you would like to disrupt the setter or make the setter play the ball.
- Establish a consistent routine prior to contacting the ball that includes your focus on where you want to direct your serve and your step(s) and toss.

TARGET SERVING

For successful, consistent serves, practice serving for control and accuracy. Along the sidelines, set up cones at the attack line, midway between the attack line and endline, and at the endline (figure 3.5). Six players per court may participate. Three servers line up behind the attack line. Three targets line up behind the attack line on the other side of the net. The targets keep their hands above their heads to give each server a visual target. The servers serve the ball to their targets, who catch the serves and roll the balls back to the servers. After five successful serves from the attack line, the servers move back to the next cone. After five successful serves there, they move back to the endline. After completing five successful serves from the endline, the servers and targets switch sides and roles.

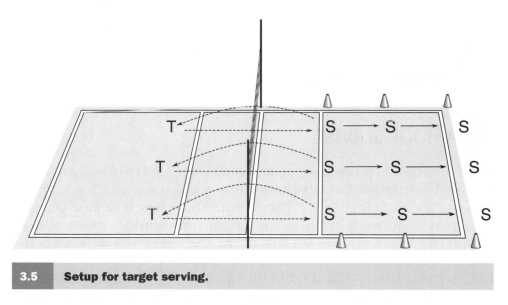

| 3.5 | Setup for target serving. |

SERVE DEEP

Once you've mastered the basic serve, it's time to practice serving for power by accelerating the hand to the ball. On each side of the net along the sidelines, place cones midway between the attack line and endline and at the endline. These cones provide a deep-court target zone for the servers. On one side of the court, 12 servers form three lines at the first cone (figure 3.6). The first server in each line attempts to serve deep into the opponent's court, then chases the serve and returns to the back of the line. After each server attempts five serves from the first cone, the servers line up behind the second cone and begin serving.

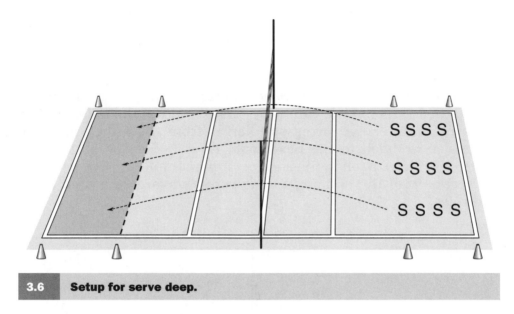

| 3.6 | Setup for serve deep. |

HULA HOOP SERVING

Serving requires more than power. Successful serving requires control and accuracy. Set up three hula hoops near the back of the opponent's court (figure 3.7). Begin with three teams of four players. One player on each team is the target and stands inside a hula hoop. The other players on his team, the servers, line up on the opposite endline. One at a time, each server attempts to serve the ball to his teammate in the hula hoop. The player in the hula hoop must catch the ball with both feet in the hoop for the team to score a point. If the serve is successful, the target runs to the back of the serving line and the server runs to the hula hoop to become the target for the next server. If the serve is unsuccessful, the server must chase down the ball and return to the end of the serving line. The first team to score 10 points wins.

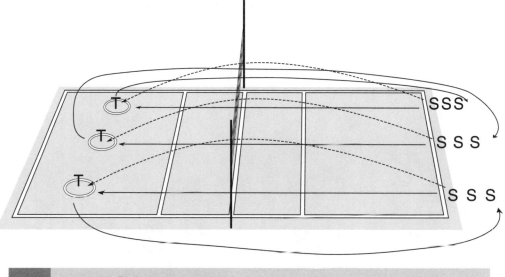

3.7 Setup for hula hoop serving.

CHAPTER

Receiving Serve

The three contact rule is unique to volleyball. It was not one of the original rules of the game, but appeared early in the sport, probably first developed in the Philippines. Let's look at these contacts one at a time, beginning with the first contact or touch by the receiving team.

The primary skill used to receive serve is a forearm pass, although you may be more familiar with the term *bumping*. The objective of the first touch in a serve reception system is to control the ball and redirect the serve to a target. Receiving the serve is often considered the most critical skill in the game. Without an effective pass, it is very difficult to execute your offense. As you begin to practice passing, it's important that you always practice passing to a target and that you practice your communication skills at the same time.

Forearm Pass

To receive a serve and execute a fore-arm pass successfully, you need to move your feet, create a platform with your arms—keeping your arms away from your body—and contact the ball with your body in a low athletic stance.

Prior to the serve, get into a ready position with your feet at least shoulder-width apart, knees bent, and hands apart (figure 4.1a). You need to be ready to move from an athletic stance to the ball. A common phrase you'll hear from coaches is "feet to ball." Even though the serve is intercepted with your forearms, your feet are a key to success in passing.

Keep your shoulders forward and your arms loose as you move to receive the serve (figure 4.1b). Do not move with your hands together. You will be able to move more quickly and

4.1   a. Ready position.

efficiently with your hands apart. Complete your movement in a slightly staggered stance with both knees bent comfortably and with your shoulders forward.

As you complete your movement, bring your hands together with your thumbs and wrists touching to create a platform (figure 4.1c). Simply grab one hand with the other and place your thumbs and wrists together with your thumbs pointing toward the floor. The key is for the arms to work as a platform, rebounding the served ball to the target.

Use every cue possible to predict where the server will direct the ball. The server may look to the zone of your court she intends to serve to, or the server's foot may point in that direction.

Your objective when you receive the ball is to guide the ball to the target. If you contact the bottom of the ball and swing your arms with a lot of force, the ball will rebound high to the rafters. If your arms make contact directly behind the ball (figure 4.1d), you can create more of a line drive pass to the target. If you arrive before the ball in a low athletic stance with your shoulders and platform aimed at your target, your chances of success improve dramatically.

The pass to the target requires good arm-eye coordination. Stay loose with your upper body and keep your arms extended. Your legs should remain stable throughout the contact phase.

4.1   b. Move to the ball.

4.1   c. Make a platform.

4.1   d. Make contact.

Praying A common error inexperienced players commit is referred to as *praying*. Prior to contact, the player brings the joined hands up near the forehead (praying position), then drops the arms near waist level to contact the ball. Players are often unaware that they make this mistake and find it hard to correct.

How do you correct this error, or any error for that matter? Often a technical error can be corrected by taking a look at the step just prior to the repeated error. I heard this tip on error correction many years ago from Sally Kus and have always remembered it as a guide to correcting mistakes. Sally is credited with more than 1,000 coaching victories with the Buffalo (New York) Cheetah volleyball club program. Imagine the number of days in practice she needed to correct players.

4.2   **Keep arms extended when passing.**

To avoid praying when passing, keep your arms extended (figure 4.2). If your arms stay extended, they can't bend, and if they can't bend, you won't develop the habit of praying before you pass.

Using Leg Drive When receiving a hard-driven serve, your legs should remain stable. The natural rebound of the ball from your arms will provide plenty of force. For a softer serve, you need to use some leg drive when the forearms contact the ball (figure 4.3). Imagine you are sitting on the edge of a chair as you get into passing position. As you contact the ball, use just enough leg drive to stand up.

4.3   **Leg drive helps repel a softer serve.**

Receiving Serve With the Hands

A recent rule change has resulted in more players receiving serve with their hands (figure 4.4). The current rule allows a double contact on any first team contact, including the use of the hands. The previous rule allowed double contact of any first team contact with the exception of hand contact. Although the intent of the rule may have been to give defenders a little more latitude against overpowering attacks, the result has been a tremendous increase in the use of the hands to receive serve. Some may argue that this rule change actually has allowed offenses to be even more effective. Regardless of differing opinions, the reality is that receiving serve with the hands is an option.

To receive serve with your hands, keep them positioned above your shoulders. Move to the ball just prior to contact with a serve to avoid a held ball. The finger pads should contact the ball.

Keep in mind that the rules of volleyball allow a double contact, not a lifted or held ball. The technical aspects of setting and overhead passing will be covered in chapter 5.

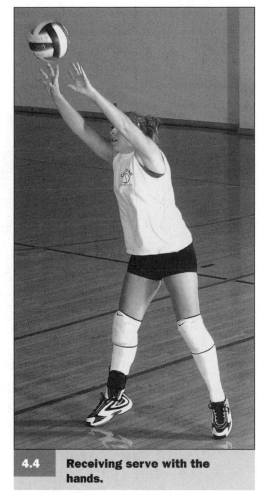

4.4 Receiving serve with the hands.

Using the Run-Through

Another passing skill is the run-through (figure 4.5). Whenever possible, move your feet to the ball and square your shoulders to the target before passing. But what happens if you can't get there in time? Run through the ball when you cannot get there before the ball. To execute a run-through, keep moving as you pass the ball.

In a game, you may need to execute a run-through for a variety of reasons. Maybe your reaction to a serve was slow, or you were fooled by the speed or location of the serve. In a two-on-two game, each player on a team covers half the court, so it is not unusual for a player to cover a lot of distance before passing. A player who is moving forward will keep the arms low while moving (figure 4.5a).

If you need to move laterally for a ball, you will find it helpful to drop your inside shoulder while moving (figure 4.5b). You can create

Run-Through

4.5   **a. Running forward.**

4.5   **b. Running laterally.**

a platform as you move for the ball and attempt to direct the ball to the target as you move and contact the ball.

Using the J-Stroke

The contact for a forward run-through may require a departure from the standard rule of keeping the platform straight when passing. If a player must run forward to play a ball near the net, it will be difficult to play the ball with a straight platform and keep it on your side of the court. The J-stroke (figure 4.6) allows backspin to be put on the passed ball to keep it on your side of the net. The J-stroke is executed by allowing a bend in the elbows as the ball is contacted. Keep your arms extended and low as you run through the ball. From a side view, the passer's arms form a J.

4.6   **J-stroke.**

Talk, Talk, Talk

It is impossible to overemphasize the importance of systematic communication in the game of volleyball. During the reception of service, players should get in the habit of first calling the ball in or out, and then an individual should take charge by calling for the ball. Team communication can be as simple as "play" or "out." The chorus of shouts from teammates indicates that all the players are anticipating the serve and making a quick judgment as to whether or not the serve will be in. Obviously, the stronger the serve, the less time available for this call to be made. It makes sense to keep all communication signals on court to short, one-syllable sounds, if possible. Individual players who intend to pass the ball either from a serve or during a rally should simply call "ball" or "mine."

Should you get in the habit of calling "yours"? Probably not. This can create confusion. Instead, use body language to show a teammate in proximity to you that you are not taking the ball. This is often referred to as opening up. If you are standing deep in the court and a strong serve is sailing out of bounds, the same idea applies. You just open up, the way a matador does when the bull rushes by, and allow the ball to sail out of bounds.

Train yourself to say "mine" or "ball" prior to every contact. Remember, communication is the key!

Give it a go: Receiving

PASS ON ONE KNEE

Passing on one knee will force you to focus on making a perfect platform and contacting the ball without moving the feet. Divide into six groups of two players each (figure 4.7). One player in each group (the tosser) stands at the net with a ball, facing his partner (the passer). Each passer kneels with one knee on the ground and forms a platform with his arms. The tosser provides an easy toss to the passer, keeping the ball near the passer's platform. The passer directs a forearm pass back to the tosser. Repeat 10 times. Players then switch positions and roles.

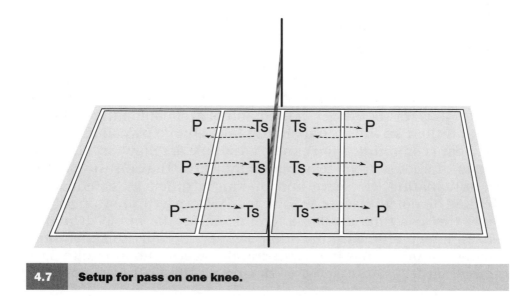

4.7   **Setup for pass on one knee.**

CORNER PASSING

The corner passing drill (figure 4.8) is a good drill for practicing passing with movement. Eight groups of two players can work on each court. Each tosser stands on a corner with a volleyball. The passer begins three meters away on one of the lines intersecting the tosser's corner. The tosser provides a toss and the passer directs a forearm pass back to the tosser. The passer quickly shuffle steps to the other line intersecting the tosser's corner, staying three meters away from the tosser, and directs another pass from a toss. Repeat for 10 round trips. Partners then switch positions and roles.

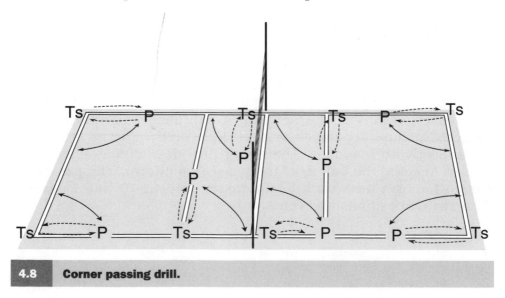

4.8   **Corner passing drill.**

TRIAD PASSING

In triad passing (figure 4.9), you will practice passing in a gamelike situation. Divide players into three teams of three. Each team needs two balls. On each team, one player is the tosser, one is the target, and one is the passer. The tosser and target both have a ball. The tosser and passer line up behind opposite attack lines, and the target lines up near the net on the passer's side. The drill begins when the tosser tosses the ball to the passer, simulating a serve. The target immediately bounces her ball to the tosser. The passer calls for the ball from the tosser and passes it to the target. Once the target has this ball, the tosser again tosses to the passer. When the passer has successfully completed 10 passes to the target, the players switch roles.

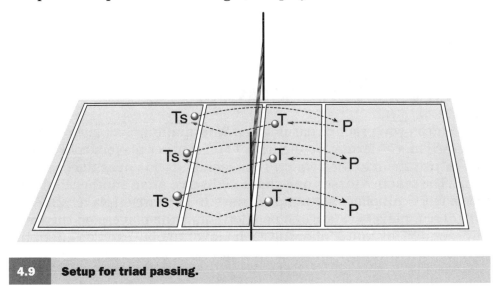

4.9 Setup for triad passing.

BUTTERFLY SERVING AND PASSING

In butterfly serving and passing (figure 4.10), you will learn to read and react to live serves by passing to the target. This is a full-court serving and passing drill. On each side is a team composed of two passers (one on the court and one waiting outside the sideline), one target near the net, and two servers (one to serve and one waiting to serve). The server serves to the passer on the opponent's side of the court, then runs to the other side to join the passing line. The passer passes to the target on his side of the court, then moves up to become the next target. The target catches the pass, then moves to the serving line. This is a continuous cycle: server to passer, passer to target, target to server. The only time a player changes sides of the court is after serving.

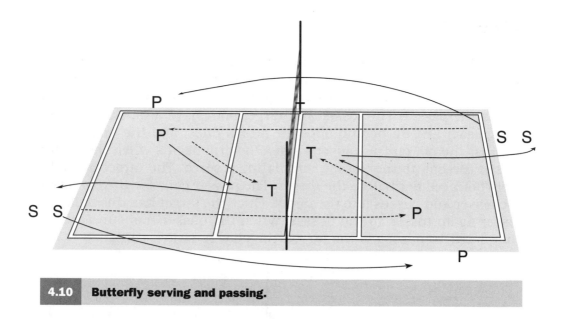

| 4.10 | Butterfly serving and passing. |

COACH VERSUS OFFENSE PASSING

In this drill, you practice passing in a W formation. Six players take to the court in a W formation (figure 4.11). Six other players collect balls and return them to the basket. The teacher stands near the basket of balls. The teacher tosses one simulated serve after another to differ- ent players. All players attempt to pass to the target (player 2). After five tosses, players rotate one position. After the players on the court have rotated six times, allowing each player to play each position, the players switch roles with those who have been collecting the balls.

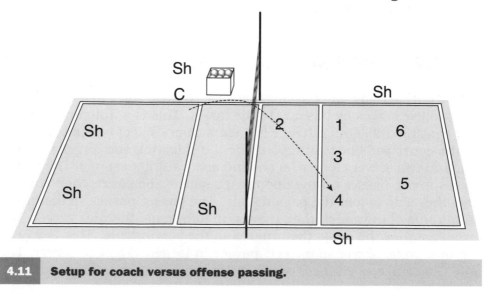

| 4.11 | Setup for coach versus offense passing. |

CHAPTER

Setting

Although it is most common to have a designated player perform the role of setter, it is important to recognize that all players will find themselves in circumstances where they need to use their hands. The rules of volleyball currently allow double contact on any first team contact, including double contact with the hands. Thus, over-head passing can be used to receive serve or free balls from an opponent, in addition to redirecting the service reception to an attacker. Once the ball has been passed to the target either with the forearms or the hands, we can refer to the set as the second touch. Since the goal is to control the ball using only three contacts, and ultimately smash the ball into the opponent's court, accuracy and consistency will obviously play an important role in setting.

Overhead Pass

The overhead pass is typically referred to as the *set*. The execution of most volleyball skills requires effective movement of players prior to contacting the ball. This is certainly true of setting.

When executing a set, focus on moving your feet to the ball (figure 5.1a) and squaring your shoulders to the target (figure 5.1b), getting your hands up quickly, forming your hands in a shape similar to the volleyball, and using the extension of your arms and legs to push the set high into the air.

To be able to square your shoulders in the direction of your intended set, you need to arrive at the spot where the ball is heading before it gets there. Once you have arrived, it is important to get your hands up quickly and have your body in an athletic stance with your feet staggered and your knees bent comfortably. It is preferable to have your right foot forward, especially if a serve reception forces you near the net.

With your hands in the shape of the volleyball (figure 5.1c), it is critical to have your thumbs pointed at your eyes. Practice this without a volleyball and you will be able to picture the ball settling into your hands quite nicely. Your goal should be to contact the ball near forehead level. As you contact the ball with your finger pads, be sure to drive with both your arms and legs in the direction of the intended set (figure 5.1d).

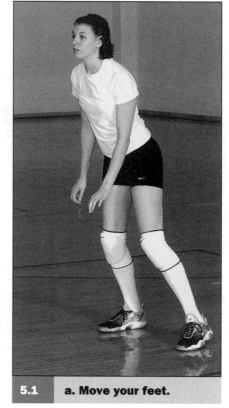

5.1   **a. Move your feet.**

5.1   b. Square your shoulders.

5.1   c. Raise your hands

5.1   d. Push the set.

Spring in the Wrists   The action of the wrists is important in the execution of a set. With your hands open and in the shape of the volleyball, your wrists will naturally give a little as the ball contacts your finger pads. This can be described as the ball going to the hands. Think of your wrists as a spring and be sure that the ball doesn't stop in your hands (figure 5.2). This would result in a held ball violation. Use the natural spring of your wrists to assist in pushing the ball back out of your hands.

One of my favorite drills to share with new learners is the spring drill. I ask a player to hold the ball in both hands in the setting position with the ball just in front of her forehead. I tell the player I am going to try to push the ball right into her forehead and that she needs to resist this force without holding onto the ball. I push hard for about two seconds, then suddenly pull my hands quickly away from the ball, and it springs right in the air. This force creates the type of tension available in the wrists for setting.

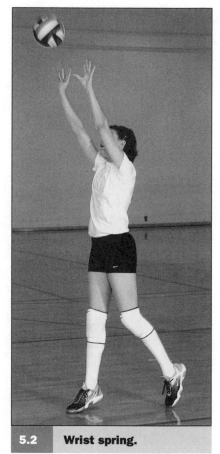

5.2   **Wrist spring.**

5.3   **Focus on your hands going to the ball.**

Making Contact   The most common setting errors involve the contact of the ball. A player may hold the ball in the hands too long and actually be whistled for a held ball infraction. I like to refer to this as the "Hhrruuummmphhh" set.

You may have heard the phrase *deep dish.* That phrase adequately describes a setter who holds the ball before releasing it. The player receives the ball with his hands near his forehead or face, holds the ball as it drops to chest level, then throws it into the air. To avoid the deep dish, think of your hands going to the ball (figure 5.3) as opposed to the ball going to your hands.

Another mistake commonly observed in setting is the slapping sound associated with a set that only contacts the palms of the hand and not the finger pads. The adjustment needed here is simply to focus on contacting the ball with the pads of the fingers (figure 5.4).

The Back Set As a setter, you are not always limited to setting to teammates in front of you. You can send the ball to eligible attackers behind you with a back set. The back set may be challenging for new players. The initial body, arm, and hand position will be helpful in execution of the back set. Contact the ball near your fore-

5.4 Make contact using your finger pads.

head, but then arch your back and drive your arms high above your head (figure 5.5). This extension should finish with your biceps near your ears. With experience and practice, you will gain confidence in setting to a player that you cannot see.

Other Uses for Setting Let's look at two more aspects of using the hands to play the ball. Receiving the serve with the hands provides an opportunity to use an overhead pass on the first touch. This can be useful on short serves or on high float serves that don't travel with a lot of force. Remember, the force of a jump

5.5 Back set.

serve could be so great that the ball comes to rest in the receiver's hands before it can be pushed out. With experience, you can anticipate and react to the type of serve used and choose whether to use the forearm pass or overhead pass to receive the serve and direct the ball to the setter.

Finally, when the opponent gives an easy free ball over the net, this is another time to contact the ball with an overhead pass, if possible. The five-person setting drill in the Give It a Go section is a practice opportunity for using the hands in several situations during a rally.

Take it to the court

Be a Designated Setter

If you are the designated setter, you first need to move, if necessary, to the agreed-upon target. Let's split the net into nine zones, numbering them from left to right (figure 5.6). You want to establish position as a target for the passers in zone 6, just to the right of the center of the net.

Your communication as the designated setter is crucial. You have a few key responsibilities in terms of effective communication. You should arrive at the target with your right shoulder near the net and your right foot forward. You should provide a visible target (right hand in the air) and a verbal signal ("here").

You will soon realize that a good percentage of passes will not arrive at the target. You must react to the pass and decide immediately if you can get to the ball and execute a set. If you decide to travel to the ball, the next key communication skill is to say "mine" as you move. Teammates need to give way when you call "mine" since it is your responsibility to get to the ball.

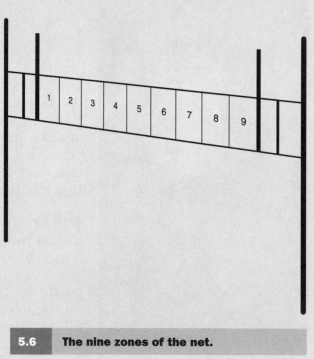

5.6 **The nine zones of the net.**

If you decide you cannot get to the ball, then the appropriate signal would be "help." The helping teammate attempts to set the ball to a teammate near one of the antennae. This is the "bread-and-butter" play for a teammate to execute when helping a setter. Your teammates must understand their responsibility to play the ball (see the bread-and-butter drill in Give It a Go). A key part of your job as the setter is the quick decision making necessary to determine whether you can execute the second touch or if you need a teammate to step in and help.

The setter needs some additional help with setting up a communication system so as to identify in advance to teammates where and how high the ball will be set. If we use the zones of the net to establish the location of the set, then we need to add a numbering system to establish the height of the set.

In figure 5.7, the three sample sets are labeled with a two-digit number. The first number identifies the location of the set along the net. The second number indicates the height. The 14 set would travel to zone 1 and would be set approximately four meters above the height of the net. The 51 set would travel to zone 5 but would be only one meter above the net. A 92 set is a back set that would travel to zone 9 with a height of two meters above the net.

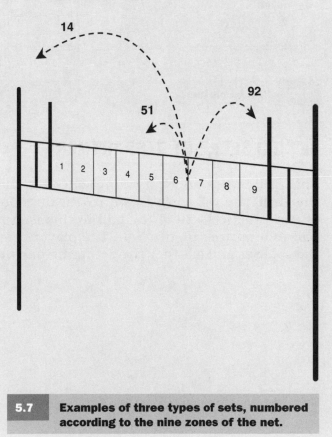

5.7 Examples of three types of sets, numbered according to the nine zones of the net.

SET TO PARTNER

In this drill, you will work on setting execution through repetition. Twenty players work with a partner, beginning 15 feet apart (figure 5.8). Each player tosses to her partner, who returns the ball with a set. Each player attempts 10 sets, then changes roles in the drill. After 10 sets, the players add five feet of distance between themselves.

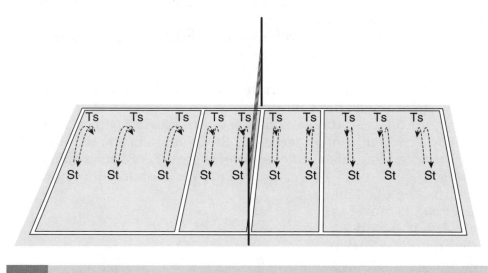

5.8 **Set to partner.**

SET TO SELF, SET TO PARTNER

This drill builds on what you practiced in the set to partner drill. In this drill, you will learn to control the direction of the set. Six groups of two practice setting the ball to themselves and then setting the ball to a partner (figure 5.9). The players can simulate a 52 set for the self-set and a 14 for the set to the partner.

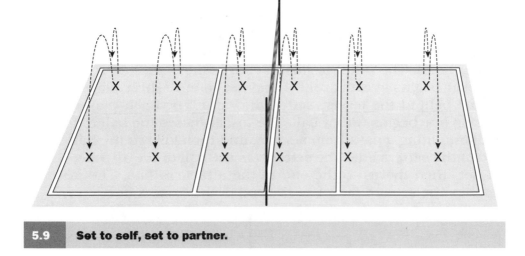

5.9   **Set to self, set to partner.**

THREE-PERSON SETTING

In the three-person setting drill (figure 5.10), you will learn to control the distance of sets and practice back sets. Four groups of three players work together, beginning about 15 feet apart. Player A on one sideline faces player B in the middle. Player C on the other sideline and player B both face player A. Player A sets the ball to player B with a front set. Player B attempts a back set to player C, who pushes the ball high in the air back to player A. The cycle is repeated 10 times. After 10 cycles, the players rotate positions. Repeat until each player has had two turns at each position.

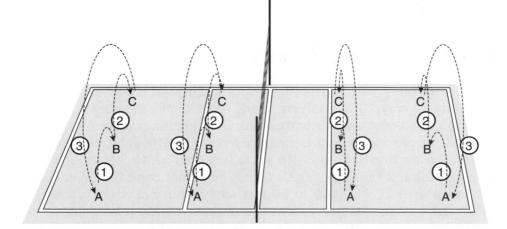

5.10   **Three-person setting.**

TRIAD SETTING

In this drill, you will practice setting 14 sets in gamelike conditions from court zone 2 and net zone 6. A total of 12 players begin in one of three lines (figure 5.11). The tosser begins in court zone 5 with a ball in hand. The setter begins in court zone 2 and net zone 6. The attacker begins in court zone 4 and net zone 1. Three players begin in line behind the tosser, setter, and attacker. Each player in the tossing line begins with a ball. The tosser tosses the ball to the setter, simulating a pass from a serve, and then follows the ball to the end of the setters line. The setter sets the ball to the attacker with a 14 set, then moves to the end of the attackers line. The attacker catches the set and moves to the end of the tossers line.

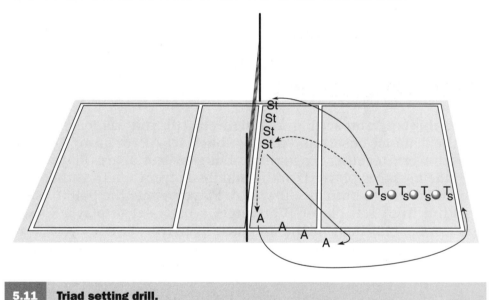

5.11 **Triad setting drill.**

FIVE-PERSON SETTING DRILL

The five-person setting drill (figure 5.12) works the overhead pass in a variety of ways. Five players work together in this drill. Player A stands near court zone 5 with a ball and begins the drill by setting the ball to player B, who is near net zone 6. The set from player A simulates an overhead pass to set a free ball to the setter. Player B gives a 92 back set to player C, who is near net zone 9. Player C sets a 14 to player D, who is 5 to 10 feet away from net zone 1. Player D takes the ball that is away from the net and sends it across the net, simulating the option of giving a free ball to the opponent with an overhead pass. Player D's set goes to player E on the opposite side of the net in zone 1. Player E sets the ball back to player A to simulate a free ball given to the opponent. This cycle is repeated five times, then each player rotates to the position of the player they were setting to. The drill continues until each player has had two opportunities in each position.

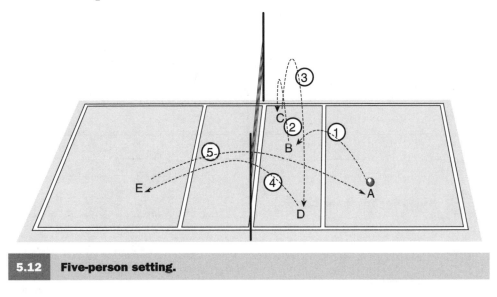

5.12 **Five-person setting.**

BREAD AND BUTTER

This drill is fundamental to developing consistent setting skills. You will practice helping a setter who calls for help on a service reception that is far away from the target. Twelve players form two lines—a line of setters (St) and a line of attackers (A). The teacher stands near the net with a basket of volleyballs (figure 5.13). The teacher tosses a ball high in the air near the middle of the court to simulate a poor service reception that would result in the designated setter having to call for help. The first player in the setting line calls "mine," while the first player in the attacking zone calls for a 14. The ball is set toward the antenna, and the attacker jumps and catches the ball with two hands high and in front of him. That player drops the ball in the basket and moves to the end of the setting line, while the setter executes the set and moves to the end of the attacking line.

Once you've mastered the basic bread-and-butter drill, try this variation. After three minutes, the two lines switch responsibilities. The setting line now attempts to set the ball high in the air for a 94 set.

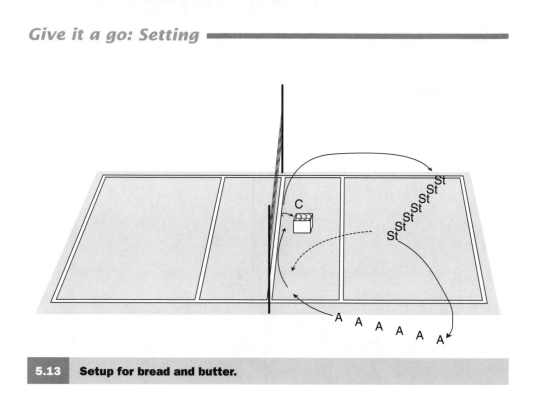

5.13 Setup for bread and butter.

6

Attacking

Run, jump, and swing. If you want to learn to attack, you need to do these three things well. The setter's job is to get a swing for an attacker on each play. The attacker's job is to anticipate and react to the set, then effectively launch herself in the air and use one of the attack options to score. We have looked at the first and second touch options; now we need to look at that third and final touch. At the highest levels of volleyball, there appears to be a clear advantage of the offense over the defense, partly because of the athletic ability of elite athletes and partly because of the myriad attack options that can be used to put the block and defense at a disadvantage. Anyone who has watched experienced players competing has probably been wowed by a spectacular spike. We literally need to take it a step at a time, so we will begin with the footwork sequence.

The Attack

As you practice the run phase of the attack, approach the net at a 45-degree angle. If you are left-handed, begin by attacking from court zone 2. If you are right-handed, begin in court zone 3 or 4. Start at the attack line and use an angled approach to the net.

Prior to your approach, your arms should hang naturally at your sides. Begin your approach at the attack line (figure 6.1a). Drive forward in a three-step sequence, beginning with a long, running step with the left foot (if right-handed. If you are left-handed, your first step will be on the right foot, second step on the left foot, third step on the right foot.). Your arms should begin to swing forward. The second running step on the right foot brings you near the net. The final step with the left foot brings you back into balance so you can jump off two feet to attack (figure 6.1b). Jumping off two feet allows you to transfer forward momentum from the run to a controlled vertical leap.

You may eventually use four steps as part of your approach, but the final three steps need to follow this sequence.

On your last two steps, incorporate a heel-toe strike with your feet. This will result in a type of braking action as you transfer from the run into a jump.

Use both arms to jump. As you move from that long first step into the two quick closing steps, your arms should swing back and then drive up into the air as you jump. Do not jump too close to the net. When you eventually swing, you will need some room to follow through.

The attacking swing requires a whiplike action of the arm, keeping the elbow above the shoulder throughout the swing, finishing with a full reach for the ball. Contact the ball with your hand high and in back of the ball. Keep the ball in front of your attacking shoulder. Snap your wrist to create topspin. The whiplike action of the arm requires a full follow-through.

Throughout the run and jump, it is crucial to judge the height and speed of the set. Keep the ball in front of you at all times. The wrist action not only puts topspin on the ball, but it also helps you avoid the block.

Two important terms to remember when attacking are *wrist away* and *cut back*. Think of wrist away as attacking in the direction of your approach and cut back as snapping your wrist back in the opposite direction from your approach.

6.1   a. Run from the attack line.

6.1   b. Jump off two feet.

Offspeed Attacks Depending on the effectiveness of the block, an offspeed attack may be a good option. The tip (figure 6.2) is a deceptive attack disguised by a strong approach and dynamic jump. Instead of swinging at the ball, reach high with a locked elbow, contacting the ball with your finger pads. Place the ball just over the blockers' hands and on the floor in open space not covered by defenders.

Another common offspeed shot is the roll shot (figure 6.3). Again, disguise this attack by completing a strong, aggressive approach. You will need to adjust your arm swing. Near the height of your jump, swing your arm in a small circle and chip the ball with an offspeed topspin motion. Tactically, the roll

6.2 **The tip.**

6.3 **The roll.**

6.4 Tooling the block.

shot is similar to the tip, as the attacker gets the ball over the block. Again, the intent is to have the ball land on the floor in front of the defenders.

Accomplished players learn that in some cases the block is the attacker's best friend. They simply beat the ball off the blocker nearest the sideline and actually aim for that blocker's outside hand. This is referred to in volleyball circles as "tooling the block" (figure 6.4) We use tools in the workshop, thus using the block to score is considered a tool.

Players who are legally positioned in the back row can also get in the act as long as they jump with both feet behind the attack line to attack a ball that is above the height of the net. Back-row players approach the attack line with the same footwork sequence. Back-row attackers can simply use "A," "B" (or "pipe"), and "C" as the verbal signals for attacks in court zones 5, 6, and 1, respectively (figure 6.5).

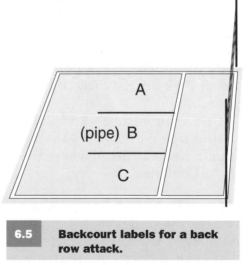

6.5 Backcourt labels for a back row attack.

Hitting a Down Ball Since we do not want to give our opponent an easy, free ball, we need to consider what we can do with a third team contact when we cannot attack; for example, if you approach the net to attack but the set ends up several feet behind you. You can't jump and swing but could adjust your footwork and step back, keeping the ball in front of you and attacking it while standing on the floor (figure 6.6). This is called a down ball. Think of it as hitting a topspin serve from the court instead of the service area. With practice, players can effectively give the opponent a tough third contact even when they can't jump and swing.

If you are not able to jump and swing at a set, you need to move behind the ball quickly. As the ball approaches, step forward with your nondominant foot and raise both arms. (This movement and body position were described in the chapter 2 in the attack against the wall activity.)

If you are right-handed, keep your left foot forward and left hand up as you whip your arm to the ball,

6.6 **Hitting a down ball.**

reaching high and snapping your wrist to create topspin. Remember, you'll have a little more court to work with if you attack deep to a corner of the opponent's court rather than down the line. A down ball or an attack from the floor often will be much more difficult for your opponent to handle than a free ball. The goal is to never give an easy free ball; replace it with a down ball whenever possible.

One other strategy to consider when you need to give your opponent a free ball is to try to make the designated setter take the first touch. Keep aware of where the opponent's designated setter is playing on defense.

Using the One-Foot Takeoff With all this talk about going off two feet, you may be wondering about the explosive attack you may have seen used by elite players with a one-foot takeoff. If a player can take a running approach along the net instead of at the net, then a one-foot takeoff can be very effective (figure 6.7). This attack is referred to as the slide. If an attacker in court zone 3 wanted to hit a 92 with a slide, he could run past the setter and use the same footwork used for a basketball layup. Use the antenna as the imaginary hoop. When the ball arrives there, take a swing at it. Often your momentum will carry you out of bounds, so quickly recover and get back on the court, ready to play.

You may encounter some challenges with mastering the attack, but now you have plenty to work on. The fundamentals for attacking are indeed fun to practice. You will see steady improvement if you master the step sequence. Adopt the mantra "left . . . right, left" if you are right-handed, "right . . . left, right" if you are left-handed. Keep the ball in front of you. Accelerate into the approach and then accelerate your arm as you put the ball to the floor. You have a lot of court to work with, so don't try to pound the ball straight down. Hit the ball with topspin deep into the opponent's court. Make your opponent try to control the ball and counterattack.

6.7 **The one-foot takeoff or slide.**

Take it to the court

It's All in the Timing

Perhaps the toughest part of attacking is the timing involved with different sets. Let's take a look at tempo and timing.

By referring back to the zones of the net and heights of sets (page 36), we can establish some basic ground rules. Students of the game often ask, "When do I leave for the attack?" That is a good question. A rule of thumb for high outside sets such as the 14 is to take all your steps after the ball is set. That keeps it simple. If that is true, then for a set like a 51, you take all your steps before the ball is set. That will be simple for the attacker but not so easy for the setter, since the quick set is a more advanced skill. Deductive reasoning should help you determine when to leave for a set like a 92. Some steps need to be taken before the ball is set and some steps after it is set.

Volleyball coaches refer to these three tempos as quick or first tempo (51), second tempo (92), and third tempo (14). Two of the attacking drills—the all the steps before drill and the all the steps after drill—will help you work on timing and tempo for attacks.

MASTERING THE APPROACH

The run phase of the attack is vital to successful attacking. This drill reinforces proper technique for the run phase. Six players begin on the attack lines of a court (figure 6.8). Righties start in court zones 3 or 4; lefties use court zone 2. All players take a full approach and simulate the arm swing on each approach. Each set focuses on a different part. Players execute five approaches for each set. Players should focus on these parts one at a time:

1. Approach the net at a 45-degree angle.
2. Focus on "left . . . right, left" or "right . . . left, right."
3. Jump off both feet.
4. Focus on using a natural arm swing.
5. Concentrate on the heel-toe braking action.
6. Jump with both arms in the air.
7. Focus on the whiplike action of the attack arm.

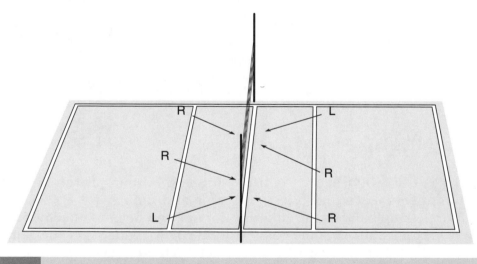

6.8   **Setup for mastering the approach.**

ALL THE STEPS BEFORE

Let's work on a first-tempo attack in which all the steps are taken before the ball is set. Six attackers begin at the attack line in court zone 3 (figure 6.9). The teacher or coach has a ball in hand and a basket of balls nearby. An attacker takes an approach and swings the arm for a 51 set. The teacher tosses the ball right to the attacker's hand for the attack. All of the attacker's steps occur before the ball is tossed to simulate the timing of a quick or first-tempo attack. The attacker chases her own attack, retrieves the ball, and places it in the basket, then gets back in line.

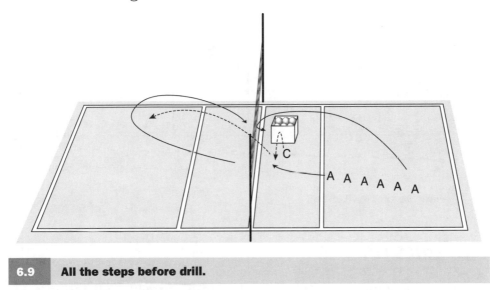

6.9 **All the steps before drill.**

ALL THE STEPS AFTER

Now we will move into a third-tempo attack in which all steps are taken after the ball is set. Six attackers begin at the attack line in court zone 4 (figure 6.10). The teacher has a ball in hand and a basket of balls nearby. The attacker leaves to attack once the teacher tosses the ball to simulate a 14 set. All the attacker's steps occur after the ball is tossed. The attacker chases her own attack, retrieves the ball, and places it in the basket, then gets back in line.

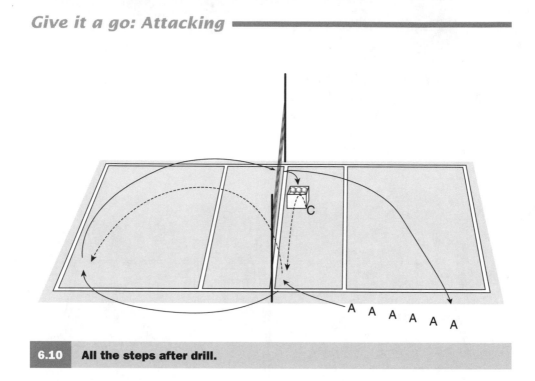

6.10 All the steps after drill.

TWO LINES HITTING

In this drill, you will practice hitting in a gamelike situation. Ten attackers start in one of two lines with a volleyball (figure 6.11). Two players set from court zone 2 and net zone 6 on either side of the net. The first attacker in each line tosses his ball to the setter and calls for a 14. The setter delivers the set, and the attacker takes a swing. The attacker retrieves the volleyball and gets in line on the other side of the net. This drill is continuous. Every two minutes two attackers switch to become setters, while the setters get in line to attack.

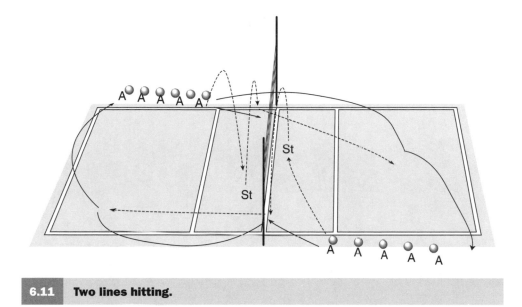

| 6.11 | Two lines hitting. |

PASS, SET, HIT

Here's your chance to practice passing, hitting, and setting, all the skills you've learned so far. Twelve players join one of three lines (figure 6.12). On one side of the net, four players are in a setting line in court zone 2 and four players are in a passing line in court zone 5. On the other side of the net, four players each have a ball and are in a line in court zone 1. The tosser tosses to the passer and moves to the end of the setting line. The passer passes the ball to the setter, calls for a 14, and approaches to attack. The setter delivers a 14 and goes to the end of the passing line. The passer completes the drill by attacking the ball, chasing and retrieving it, and going to the tossing line. This drill continues for a timed period or until each player has had 20 attempts to pass and swing.

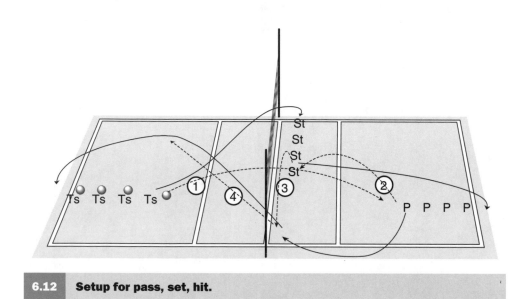

6.12 Setup for pass, set, hit.

Blocking

Domination of an opponent in volleyball is most likely to result from either service aces or uncontested attacks. The attacker is on the offensive. The attacker knows in advance the height and location of the set and is poised to drive the ball to the floor. The first line of defense against this attack is the block. Blockers have several basic responsibilities. The first priority is to avoid giving up uncontested attacks. The front-row defenders need to identify which attacker they have primary responsibility for, stay in front of that attacker as they approach the net, and get their hands over the net in front of the attacker's arm. Think of these duties in three parts: see the hitter, front the hitter, and seal the net.

A second priority is for a blocker or a group of blockers working together to put up a wall of hands in front of an attacker. Blockers always hope to intercept the attack with their hands, but it is equally important for team defense that the individual or collective block takes a portion of the court away from the attacker based on their positioning. If the block can channel the attack to portions of the court, then the team can place defenders in those areas. We will build on these concepts in chapter 9, Team Defense. For now, let's start by getting the block in front of the hitters.

The Block

All three front-row defenders need to be within an arm's length of the net at the moment their teammate serves the ball. Blockers should stand in ready position with their hands above shoulder level, knees slightly bent, and toes pointed directly at the centerline (figure 7.1a). Keep in mind that your opponent has three basic front-row attack options—left, middle, and right. All three blockers need to identify those three players and assume primary responsibility for the adjacent attacker.

To execute a block from the ready position, simply bend your knees, keeping your hands open and in the same position above your shoulders, and explode into the air (figures 7.1b and c). Your goal should be to get both hands across the plane of the net and then land in a controlled, cushioned landing by keeping your knees bent (figure 7.1d).

7.1   **a. Ready.**   **b. Bend knees, hands open and up.**

As the attacker approaches the net, the blocker should attempt to use side shuffle steps to stay in front of the hitter. Any movement should end with the blocker back in the balanced ready position, prepared to jump off both feet. The blocker's cardinal rule for timing is to jump only after the attacker jumps. The blocker's hands need to be open and strong and should always be facing zone 6 of the opponent's court. Blockers should keep their thumbs close to each other, allowing their hands to work as a unit and surround the ball.

Blocking is a key skill to successful volleyball. Your blocking skill may make the difference between winning or losing, between grabbing or sustaining the momentum for your team or giving up the momentum to your opponents.

c. Explode up.   d. Land softly.

Learn the skills and techniques of blocking and practice them. Your team will be better for it.

Watching for Cues   What does the blocker watch throughout the blocking sequence? At first glance, you might think blockers simply need to watch the ball, ending up with their hands in front of the ball. Although that will often work, a more effective strategy is to begin watching the ball as soon as it is contacted by the receiving team. Remember, the pass may come right over the net.

If the ball is passed to the setter, then focus on the ball in the setter's hands, since the setter has the option of sending it over the net. Once the setter sends the ball to an attacker, watch the ball long enough to determine where it will end up, then focus on the attacker. The eye sequence for the blocker is to watch the ball as it is passed, watch the ball in the hands of the setter, watch the set ball just long enough to know where it will end up, then watch the attacker. You can shorten these key ideas to "ball, setter, ball, hitter" to use as a reminder when blocking.

An additional advantage of watching the hitter just prior to the block is that the blocker is the first one to see the arm action of the attacker. This is especially important if the attacker chooses to use a tip or a roll shot.

Getting the Hands Over the Net   A blocker's most common challenges involve getting the hands over the net. Blockers should always keep their hands in front of their face and head to avoid moving their arms and hands behind their head when jumping. This movement results in throwing the hands at and onto the net. Simply be sure that at any point in the block you can see the backs of your hands (figure 7.2). If you can't see the backs of your hands, they are in the wrong place.

It is perfectly legal to reach over the net to block. You just need to let the attacker have the first chance to touch the ball on her side of the net.

7.2   **Watch your hands.**

The ideal block is one that results in the ball being contacted on the opponent's side of the net and going straight down on that side. Players refer to this as a *roof*. The angle of the arms reaching over the net should simulate the angle of a roof on a house (figure 7.3). In most cases, even at the highest levels of the game, the blockers don't dominate at the net, so the position of the block is just as important and maybe even more important than those rally-ending roofs.

Using the Soft Block

What about players who cannot reach

7.3 **Making the roof.**

7.4 **Soft block.**

over the net? They can still be effective by establishing good position for a multiple block. Additionally, a vertically challenged player can use a soft block by positioning his hands a few inches from the net with wrists cocked back, similar to a setting position (figure 7.4). An attacked ball contacting strong blocking hands placed in this position will often rebound high into the air and to a backcourt defender on the blocker's team. This contact does not count as a team or individual contact, so the blocker has been effective at slowing down the ball and keeping it in play.

Group Blocking

Although a blocker may need to execute a single block without help, multiple players may also work together to block. A group block is most common on a ball set to net zone 1 or zone 9, what we refer to as an outside set or a set near the antennae. The outside blocker (right front or left front player) is responsible for establishing the position of a multiple-player block by using quick shuffle steps to front the hitter. To move to the left, simply step left with your left foot and close with a step to the left with your right foot. To move to the right, step right with your right foot and close with a step to the right with your left foot.

The middle blocker not only has primary responsibility for the opponent's middle attacker, but also must watch for outside sets and attempt to join her teammate to put up a wall of hands. This sideways movement will require more than short shuffle steps. Side-to-side movement of blockers requires short runs along the net, ending with a blocker in a balanced position, ready to jump with the outside blocker just after the attacker has left the ground. This can best be performed by using a step, crossover step, closing step pattern. To crossover step to the left, take a short step to the left with your left foot, cross your right foot in front of your left foot, then step to the left again with your left foot. To crossover step to the right, take a short step to the right with your right foot, cross your left foot in front of your right foot, then step to the right again with your right foot.

An outside blocker may also use crossover steps if he needs to travel more than a few feet to either side. A middle blocker can add a side shuffle step to the end of the crossover step pattern if he needs to make a small final adjustment to end up shoulder to shoulder with his teammate.

The middle blocker is responsible for closing the space between the two blockers and relies on the outside blocker to establish the position of the multiple block. The middle blocker's goal is to have his outside foot end up four to six inches from the outside foot of the outside blocker.

Both blockers keep their hands facing the opponent's court zone 6, especially the outside blocker. Remember, the attacker could be looking to tool the block, and the outside hand of the outside blocker is an inviting target.

One of my coaches used to say that team sports require athletes to go directly from one job to the next, and this is true for the blocker. Blockers need to be prepared to keep playing after executing a block. Many attacks end up going past or over the block, and the blocker should try to track the ball with her eyes even as it goes past her. If her head follows her eyes, and if her body follows her head, then the blocker would naturally turn toward her own backcourt teammates as she lands, just in case a ball is dug and comes right back at the blocker. The block and turn drill trains a player for this situation.

Finally, a word about communication. Prior to the serve, each blocker should signal to his teammates the uniform numbers of the opposing front-row players who are eligible attackers. Outside blockers can also give a "right here" cue to the middle blocker once they have made their final adjustment steps to get in front of a hitter. This helps the middle blocker, since he is following the "ball, setter, ball, hitter" sequence. The middle blocker may have time to peek at the outside blocker, but hearing the outside blocker is helpful. When the middle blocker arrives with the outside blocker before the attacker leaves the ground, the outside blocker can give the timing cue "ready, go" to make sure both players jump at the same time.

A beach or grass court blocker playing in a two-on-two match often signals the server with one or two fingers behind the back prior to service. One finger indicates "I'm blocking line"; two fingers means "I'm blocking angle."

ON THE FLOOR BLOCKING

When you block, you need to surround the ball with your hands. For this drill, 12 players work in pairs using any available court space. Stand on the floor across from your partner, reaching high and in front of your body with your hands in the blocking position. You partner holds a volleyball with her nondominant hand within six inches of your hands and attacks the ball with her dominant hand into the block. Both of you stay on the floor throughout the drill. As the blocker, you should attempt to surround the attacked ball with your hands and keep your eyes on the ball.

BALL EXCHANGE

It's important to practice reaching over the net. For the ball exchange, 8 players form pairs and stand across the net from each other. You should attempt to match up with a player who is similar in size and jumping ability. One of you starts with the ball in both hands and jumps, raising the ball above the height of the net, and the other should reach over the net to take the ball out of the jumper's hands. This action will simulate the blocking action of reaching over the net. Each pair needs to exchange the ball back and forth over the net 10 times in a row.

MIRROR DRILL

In the mirror drill (figure 7.5), you will practice fronting the hitter. Six players work in pairs at the net. Three players begin on the attack line, each with a blocker across the net in front of them in a ready position. Each attacker needs to take a quick approach to either side of the blocker. The attacker approaches and takes a simulated swing. The blocker reacts to the movement of the attacker and uses side shuffle steps to get in front of the hitter and jump to block just after the attacker leaves the ground. Each attacker must approach 10 times; then the attackers switch positions and roles with their partner.

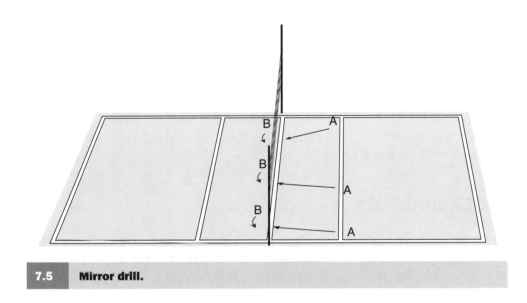

7.5 **Mirror drill.**

SIDE-TO-SIDE SHUFFLE

Effective blocking requires that you move. In this drill, you will practice using side shuffle steps to the left and right. Eight blockers form two lines in court zone 4 on each side of the net. The first player in each line assumes the ready position for blocking and takes a side shuffle and close step to their right, followed by a block. This is repeated two more times as the player travels toward the other sideline and then moves to the back of the line opposite from where they started. The drill continues until each player has taken two complete trips on each side of the net. The drill can be extended by restarting with both lines in court zone 2; all players will then move to their left for two complete trips on each side of the net.

STEP, CROSSOVER STEP, AND CLOSE

This drill continues to work on movement except you will practice the step, crossover step, and close pattern to the left and right (for middle blockers). Eight blockers form two lines in court zone 4 on each side of the net. The first player in each line assumes the ready position for blocking and takes a step, crossover step, and close step to their right, followed by a block. This is repeated one more time as the player travels toward the other sideline and then moves to the back of the line opposite from where they started. Continue the drill until each player has taken two complete trips on each side of the net. The drill can be extended by restarting with both lines in court zone 2; all players will then move to their left for two complete trips on each side of the net.

BLOCK AND TURN

After attempting to block the ball, you need to turn and get ready for the next play. Four players form a line in court zone 4, prepared to attack a 14 (figure 7.6). Four other players form a line near court zone 2. The first player in this line assumes the ready position, and on the coach's command to block, executes a simulated block attempt. The blocker turns toward the coach as soon as possible after the block, takes the toss from the coach, and sets a 14 to the first attacker in line. The attacker swings, attacks, chases the ball, places it in the basket, then goes to the end of the blocking line. The blocker moves to the attacking line after setting. The drill continues for a timed period or until each player has done a certain number of repetitions.

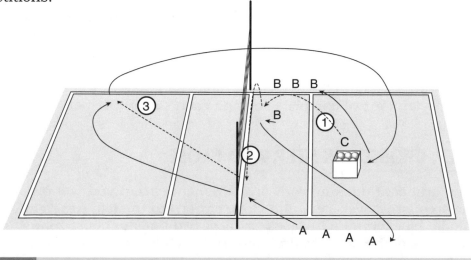

7.6 Block and turn.

CHAPTER

Digging

Often when we watch volleyball we are thrilled by the diving, rolling saves that players make when they hit the floor. But that is not where we want to start. We need to begin by working on retrieving the attack that is hit right at us. If a team has to rely on fantastic and exciting saves made by players leaving their feet, they are in trouble. Yes, those great plays can turn around the momentum of a game, and they are critical, but the foundation of effective digging has to begin with defensive positioning and technique that allows a player to stay on his feet, keep the ball off the floor, and better yet, control the ball on his own side of the net so the defense can transition to offense with a counterattack.

The Dig

Stay low—two simple words to keep in mind when your opponent has the ball and you are not involved in the block. The attacked ball is going to go to the floor, so that is where you need to be, near the floor. To be ready to dig, you need be in a wide stance with your feet more than shoulder-width apart (this will get you low); have your shoulders forward, and keep your hands apart and away from your body, both in front of and outside your hips (figure 8.1a).

It is essential to keep your arms apart in the ready position so you will be prepared to dig a ball hit to either side of your body. If you put your arms together and move them as a unit, your contact with the ball will likely result in the ball flying off the court in the direction your arms were moving.

The key idea to remember when digging is to absorb. The attack often has some heat on it. The attacker will be trying to snap her wrist and put the ball on the floor. Your goal is to put or keep your body behind the attacked ball. Your hands and arms will form a platform similar to what you have practiced with passing (figure 8.1b). However, your arms will be near your body as you contact the ball. This will help you absorb the shock of the attack.

As you dig the ball, relax your shoulders and draw them back as your hips move forward. This body action will help you absorb the speed of the attack (figure 8.1c) and allow the rebounding dig to stay on your side of the net. In fact, as you practice absorbing the attack, you will see that the proper arm and body positions result in backspin on the dug ball. This is exactly what you want, since that backspin will help keep the ball in the air on your side of the net.

Don't be surprised if you have very little time to communicate with teammates prior to digging a ball. Do your best to call "mine" so a teammate is aware that you can play the ball. Additionally, try to call "tip" whenever you see an attacker using an offspeed shot. Limited reaction time creates a great challenge for communication on defense, so work on your ability to anticipate what the offensive player intends to do.

8.1   a. Ready position.

8.1   b. Make a platform.

8.1   c. Absorb the attack.

Digs to the Side To dig a ball hit just out of your reach on either side, you only need to move one arm. Drop the inside shoulder of the arm away from the ball and bring that arm and hand together with your other arm and hand to make your platform (figure 8.2). If you combine this movement with a lateral shift of weight, attempting to get your hips behind the attacked ball, you will discover that your arms will be ready to keep the ball in play instead of having it head out of bounds.

8.2 Dig to the side.

Executing the Run-Through Players receiving a tip will need to move forward to play the ball by using a run-through. Run-throughs were discussed in chapter 4 on receiving serve (page 26), but this skill also is an important part of individual defense. When you play defense, always anticipate the attack. Keep your body in low position. Stay low as you execute the run-through. Standing up straight and running will cost you valuable time in getting to the ball. Start low and stay low as you move, with your arms extended in front of you as you execute the defensive run-through.

Using the Sprawl Our focus to this point has been on the goal of digging the ball and remaining on your feet. In certain situations, though, you need to leave your feet and go to the floor to make a save. Let's consider these situations emergencies. An emergency indicates the need for urgent action. Diving, rolling, or sprawling on the floor all qualify as urgent actions on the volleyball court. Diving and rolling are advanced floor emergency skills that can easily cause injury if executed incorrectly. Let's look at a skill that will allow you to collapse to the floor from your defensive ready position—the sprawl.

The purpose of the sprawl is to be able to step and slide forward to cover ground quickly. The sprawl can be an effective skill to use if an attacker uses a tip or a roll shot or if the ball comes off the block and begins to fall just behind the blockers and in front of a defender.

To practice the sprawl, assume the defensive ready position (figure 8.3a). In slow motion, step forward with one foot, keeping both elbows inside your knees (figure 8.3b). Simply walk yourself forward on your hands until you are on the ground. Repeat this again, but this time concentrate on the position of your legs. The leg you are pushing off with as you walk yourself forward should end up straight when you are on the floor. You will be stepping with the opposite foot, so be sure that the leg of the stepping foot hits the floor on the inside of the knee. This leg needs to end up in a bent position when you are on the floor. Continue this little drill until you can walk yourself forward on your hands and end up with the pushing leg straight and the stepping leg bent.

The final step in this progression is to get low, take the step, and slide forward with the outside part of your hands along the ground. This movement is not a crash to the floor but rather a collapse (figure 8.3c).

It won't take long to get comfortable going to the floor. Add a quick, running step once you feel confident. As you step, simulate the action of digging a ball in front of you just before you collapse and sprawl forward. The defensive skill is the contact of the ball on your arms, and the sprawl is the emergency or the recovery skill; that is, the ability to get yourself safely to the floor once you have let your body go off balance and left your feet. This is true of any emergency skill—the defensive skill is contacting the ball, and the skill that allows you to land safely and get back on your feet is the recovery from that action.

When the ball is way out of your range, you can use the sprawl to slide across the floor and extend your hand, palm down, across the floor. By sliding your hand just under a ball that is inches from striking the floor, you can make an exciting save. The ball will pop back in the air off the back of your hand. This is called a pancake. Clearly, this is a last-resort technique, but with practice, you will be prepared to react instantly in a situation that seems hopeless and keep the ball off the floor.

8.3 **a. Defensive ready position.**

8.3 **b. Step forward, elbows inside knees.**

8.3 **c. Fall gently to the floor.**

Can You Dig It?

Don't get confused by the ready position or body position during contact. If you assume the contact position before the ball is attacked, you will find yourself with your weight back on your heels. This will mean trouble for any situation in which the attacker decides to use an offspeed shot (the tip and roll shots). Keep those shoulders forward prior to contact as you read the attacker's shoulders and consider the angle of his approach. These cues will help you anticipate where he may attack. You need to place yourself outside the area of the court taken away by the block in front of you. You want to get a good look at the attacker, so don't play behind the blockers. Be sure to move where you can see the attacker.

PEPPER

Pepper (figure 8.4) is a good way to work on ball control skills, including digging. Players work in pairs. Player 1 starts by attacking at player 2, who digs the ball back to player 1. Player 1 then sets the ball to player 2, who attacks at player 1. Player 1 then digs to player 2, who sets the ball back to player 1. This is the end of one cycle. The drill continues until players have attempted to complete 10 cycles without an error or for a specified time period.

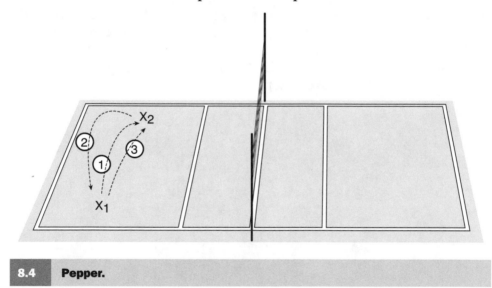

8.4   **Pepper.**

ONE-LINE DIGGING

Six players form one line near court zone 5 to practice digging (figure 8.5). Four players help by shagging volleyballs during the drill and placing them in the basket. One player serves as a feeder by feeding balls to the teacher or coach throughout the drill. One player serves as the target for the diggers. The first digger in line assumes the defensive ready position and digs the attack from the teacher back to the target. The digger then returns to the end of the digging line. Each player has 10 attempts, then the six diggers switch roles with the other six players.

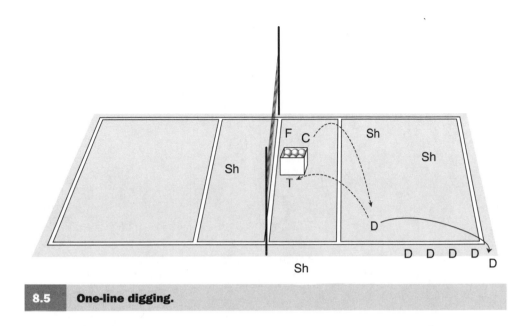

8.5 **One-line digging.**

DEFENSE VERSUS BACK-ROW ATTACK

Gamelike situations are the best way to practice. This drill allows players to practice digging while moving through situations they will see in a game. Three players line up on side A in court zones 5, 6, and 1, with another player positioned behind each of them but off the court behind the endline (figure 8.6). One player stands near the net as a target for the diggers on side A. Three players on side B take court zone positions 5, 6, and 1, with another player behind each of them. These players are the attackers. One player is the setter on side B. A teacher or coach stands off the court near court zone 5 with a basket of balls nearby. The teacher tosses a ball to the setter. The setter can set an A, B, or C back-row attack. The attacker hits deep into side A and moves into one of the digging lines on side A. The defensive players react to the ball, and one player digs the ball to the target. The digger becomes the next target. The target retrieves the ball, places it in the basket, and moves to side B to become a back-row attacker. Every two minutes, a new player is selected to be the setter.

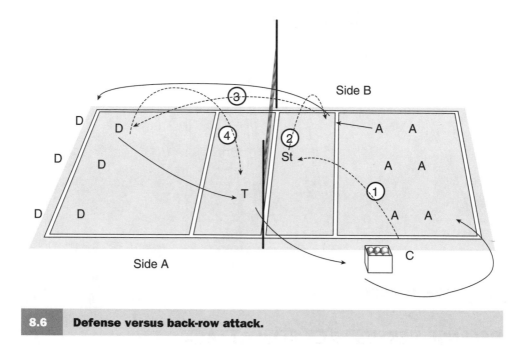

8.6 **Defense versus back-row attack.**

SERVE AND DIG

Now you have the chance to practice defense in a gamelike situation. Set up three cones in the backcourt on the serving side, one near each sideline and one near the endline toward the middle (figure 8.7). Place a basket of volleyballs near the net. A teacher or coach, who will act as an attacker, stands near the basket of balls. Six servers line up behind the endline, and five other players stand ready to chase the volleyballs and return them to the servers and teacher. One player serves as a target. The first server executes a serve, then moves in front of one of the cones. The teacher hits the ball to the server to simulate an attack, and the server digs the attack from the teacher back toward the basket of balls. The teacher should continue to use volleyballs from the basket. The server returns to the end of the line of servers as the next player serves. After five minutes, the players switch roles.

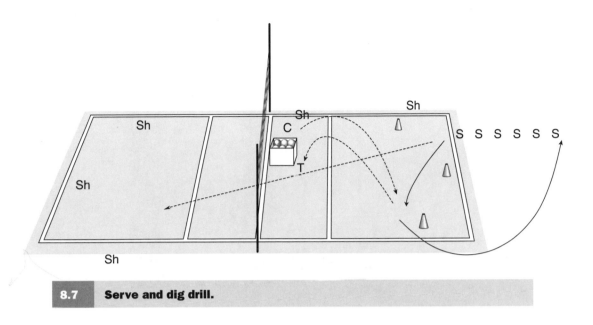

8.7   **Serve and dig drill.**

Team Defense

Where's your base on defense? If it is important to have a starting position on offense, then it is equally important to have a starting point on defense. In volleyball, this is referred to as *base position.*

Always keep one thing in mind when playing defense: The ultimate objective is to keep the ball off the floor and on your side of the net. A good goal would be to dig the ball high in the air near the middle of the court to allow time for your defensive teammates to transition to their offensive positions. The tendency is to dig every ball to the target (court zone 2 and net zone 6). The danger in making this your target for defense is that a ball dug just a foot or two over the net makes a wonderful gift for your opponent. Attackers can blast a poorly controlled dig right back at you. It is better to be less accurate with digs away from the target than over the net.

First or Second Contact

To keep team defense simple, each front-row player needs to stand within an arm's length of the net in the ready blocking position. The back-row players form a triangle (figure 9.1a).

When we think of team defense, we tend to start by thinking about how we will handle the ball set to an attacker, but that is getting ahead of ourselves. Once the serve is put in play, each defensive player must find the ball as it is being received by the opponent and be ready to react if the ball is returned immediately over the net. The overpass may not be what your opponent intends, but it happens, and the defense must be prepared to respond. This is the first opportunity for a defensive play.

The blockers have the first chance to play the ball and must prepare to defend against the overpass. A blocker can block the ball, attack the ball, or step back and bring it under control with a pass (figures 9.1b, c, and d).

If the ball travels over the blockers' heads, then the back-row defenders get to play defense. The back-row defenders must have the entire court covered, as shown in the shaded triangle. The players in court zones 1 and 5 can take any ball that comes over the net near the middle of the court. The player in court zone 6 can cover the deep areas of the court.

When your opponent passes the ball to a setter, the defense must prepare for the opponent's second touch to be directed over the net, either intentionally or unintentionally. The blocker must be ready to play the ball at the net. Blockers should look at the setter when the ball is in the setter's hands. The setter has the option of dumping the ball over with one hand, two hands, or even with a jump and tip or swing if the setter is a legal front-row player. The base position of your blockers and defenders enables them to defend this situation.

We have looked at how front- and back-row defenders should handle the opponent's first or second touch if it is directed over the net. Now we are ready to move on to the concepts involving the blockers and defenders working together as a unit.

Most of the time when an opponent uses all three contacts, the final touch will be an attack. From the base position, a team can defend against an opponent's attack from court zones 4, 2, and 3. We will refer to this defensive system as "middle back" since the defender in court zone 6 stays deep.

The blockers are positioned to take the middle of the court away from the attacker. Their block attempts to force the attacker to hit around them. Their defensive teammates move into areas of the court not taken away by the blockers.

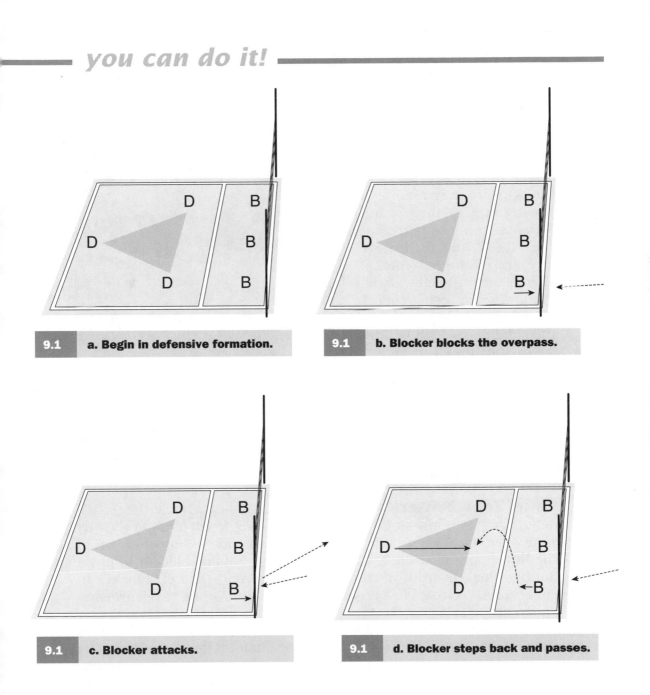

9.1 a. Begin in defensive formation.

9.1 b. Blocker blocks the overpass.

9.1 c. Blocker attacks.

9.1 d. Blocker steps back and passes.

Court Zone 4 Attack

Against a court zone 4 attack, the outside blocker stays in front of the hitter, and the middle blocker joins the outside blocker to put a double block in front of the attack (figure 9.2). The off-blocker in court zone 4 doesn't stay at the net but retreats to a position near the attack line to retrieve any sharp-angle attacks. The defender directly behind the blocker in court zone 1 moves from base position to the sideline to dig a ball hit down the line. This player also must be ready to protect against any tips over the block. The crosscourt de-

9.2 **Defending a court zone 4 attack.**

fender in court zone 5 moves against the sideline to defend the crosscourt attack. The player in court zone 6 stays deep in the court behind the block to cover any ball that comes over the block or travels deep down either sideline.

Court Zone 2 Attack

To defend a court zone 2 attack, the team's defensive positioning mirrors the positioning for defending a court zone 4 attack. The outside blocker in court zone 4 stays in front of the hitter, and the middle blocker joins the outside blocker to put a double block in front of the attack (figure 9.3). The off-blocker in court zone 2 retreats to a position near the attack line to retrieve any sharp-angle attacks.

The defender directly behind the blocker in court zone 5 moves from base position to the sideline to dig a ball hit down the line. This player also must be ready to protect against any tips over the block. The crosscourt defender in court zone 1 moves against the sideline to defend the crosscourt attack. The player in court zone 6 stays deep in the court behind the block to cover any ball that comes over the block or travels deep down either sideline.

9.3 Defending a court zone 2 attack.

Court Zone 3 Attack   To defend a court zone 3 attack, the middle blocker takes solo responsibility for blocking (figure 9.4). Both off-blockers move in a low position near the attack line to defend against tips, rolls, or balls deflected off the blocker's hands. The two wing defenders in zones 1 and 5 guard their sidelines. The player in court zone 6 stays deep to cover any ball hit over the block or deep into the corners.

9.4 Defending a court zone 3 attack.

Back-Row Attack   Do you remember the back-row attack option introduced in chapter 6? Legally positioned players in the back row can attack as long as they jump with both feet behind the attack line to attack a ball above the net. Defending the back-row attack presents a new challenge.

The blocker in front of the attacker must delay his jump slightly since the ball is being attacked from the backcourt. Compared to an attack near the net, the back-row attack takes a little longer to clear the net. The blocker's timing is important on this play. The three back-row defenders all move deep, and the two front-row players who are not involved in the block should move to a low position near the attack line to defend against deflected attacks or offspeed shots (figure 9.5). The middle up defense against the back-row attack would remain the same. All three back-row defenders would stay deep.

These are the basic defensive positions and tactics for a middle back defense. Every defense has a weakness; the middle of the court is vulnerable with this type of defense. Players must guard the perimeter of the court first and move to retrieve any ball hit in front of them. The game of volleyball requires anticipation. Players must be able to read what the opponent is doing and react to each situation.

9.5   **Defending a back-row attack.**

Offspeed Attack   At times, an opponent may try to gain the upper hand with an offspeed attack against a middle back defense (figure 9.6). In this case, the defense can easily adjust. The player in court zone 6 should move behind the middle blocker on every play. This player should stay just behind the attack line so he can see the attacker's hands. The court zone 6 player is responsible for all tips and roll shots.

The wing defenders should move deeper along their sidelines since they no longer have responsibility for moving to cover offspeed attacks. The middle back part of the court will be vulnerable, placing added responsibility on the blockers to take this part of the court away from the attacker.

Middle Up Defense

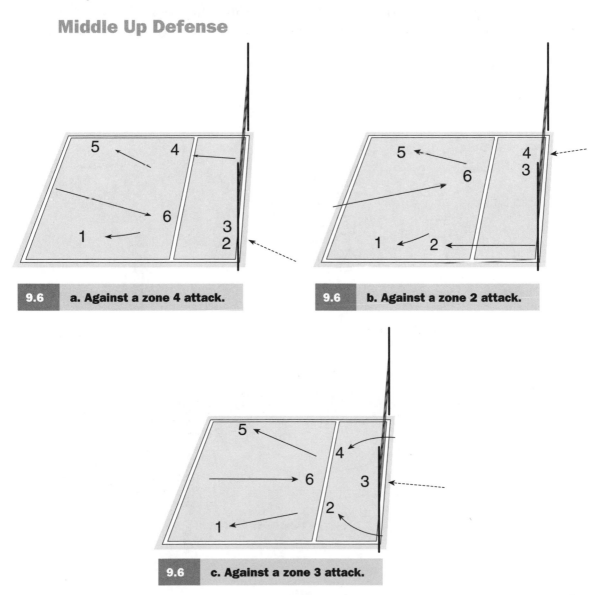

| 9.6 | a. Against a zone 4 attack. |

| 9.6 | b. Against a zone 2 attack. |

| 9.6 | c. Against a zone 3 attack. |

Defensive Specialization

Specialization in volleyball represents a step up from introductory play to a more advanced level. But just imagine how you'll be able to skunk your cousins at the next family reunion!

We have built on the simple W formation introduced in chapter 1 by adding communication signals for each skill and communication systems such as court zones and play sets. Specialization is another way to enhance the level of play on the court. Let's go back and look at the base formation and assign positions to each player. First, we will assign uniform numbers to the six players and identify where they begin on the court and what positions they play. Figure 9.7 shows the first rotation and figure 9.8 shows the second rotation.

Rotation 1

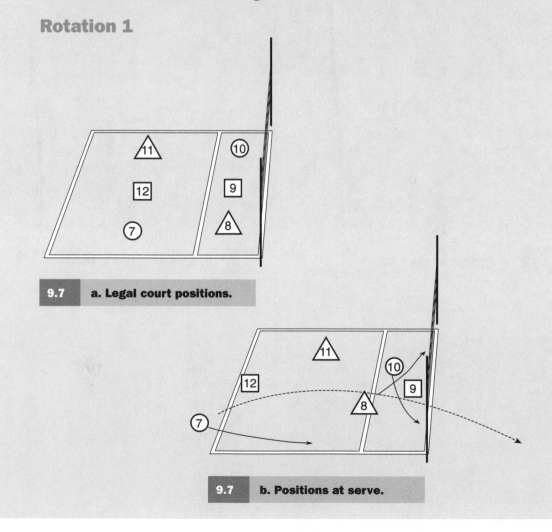

9.7   **a. Legal court positions.**

9.7   **b. Positions at serve.**

Notice that in the legal initial court positions, left-side players (triangles) begin opposite each other in the rotation. Two designated middles (squares) also begin opposite each other, as do the setters/right-side players (circles). Remember, players must be in legal court positions at the moment of service. In the initial court position, players 10 and 8 are as close to each other as legally possible. They keep to either side of player 9 at the moment of serve, but since they know they will be switching, they prepare for the switch by planning for the shortest possible movement to their defensive positions.

At the serve, player 10 moves to court zone 2 and player 8 moves to court zone 4. This switch puts the team into specialized positions. Both triangles are now on the left side, both squares are in the middle, and the setters/right-side players are both on the right.

Keep in mind that at the end of each rally, players must return to their legal court positions prior to the next serve.

Rotation 2

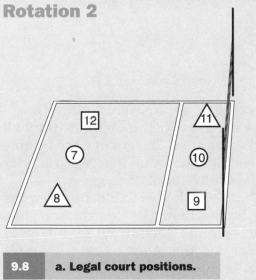

9.8   **a. Legal court positions.**

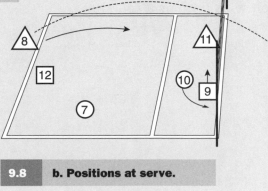

9.8   **b. Positions at serve.**

The Libero

Recent rules changes in volleyball have resulted in the adoption of a new position called a *libero*. You may have observed a collegiate or international match where one player on each team wears a uniform of a contrasting color to the rest of the team. The libero is a back-row specialist. Defense is a big part of the libero's role on the court. The libero can come into the backcourt for any player but is not allowed to serve, participate in a block, set a ball to a teammate if in front of the attack line, or attack a ball above the height of the net.

One reason for introducing the libero was to give shorter players a bigger role in the game, but the ability to play this position need not be limited by the height of the player. An effective libero is a strong ball control player who is able to focus on the skills of passing and defending, just as many front-row substitutions are able to focus on blocking and attacking.

Defensive Teamwork

Team defense requires a lot of discipline because each player has a predetermined area of responsibility. However, sometimes the ball is attacked in the seam between two players. Players need to be able to work together so they do not collide. The seam digging drill later in the chapter illustrates this type of situation.

You may see teams use more than two players to block. Typically, a triple block is used only at elite levels of play. As you can imagine, six hands in front of a hitter can be quite effective in taking away part of the court from the attacker. On the other hand, it exposes more undefended area that could be inviting for an attacker to exploit with a tip or a roll shot.

DEFENSE VERSUS ONE LINE OF ATTACKERS

Let's practice moving from base position to defensive position against a left-side attack. Four attackers line up on the attack line near court zone 4 (figure 9.9). A teacher or coach on the same side of the net initiates the drill by tossing a ball to the player designated as the setter for the drill. Six defenders on the other side of the net begin in base positions. As the ball is set, the defenders move into proper position for a middle back defense and attempt to stop the attack with a block or dig. After each play, the attacker and six defenders rotate one court position. The attacker moves under the net to block in zone 3. All defenders rotate one position to defend against the next attacker. The player in court zone 4 retrieves the ball after each play, returns it to the ball basket, then joins the attacking line. Different players should be rotated into the setting position every two minutes.

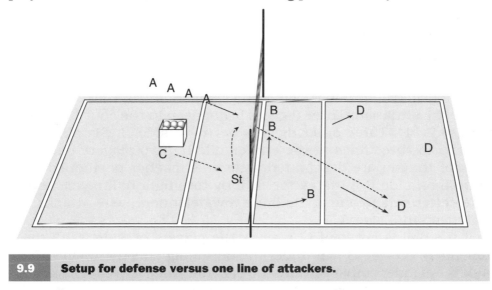

9.9 Setup for defense versus one line of attackers.

SEAM DIGGING

In the seam digging drill (figure 9.10), adjacent defenders practice moving to cover a ball hit in the seam. Four players begin in a blocking line near court zone 4. Four other players form a digging line near court zone 5. The first blocker and defender in line begin in base position. When the teacher near court zone 2 tosses the ball in the air, both defenders move to their middle back defensive positions and prepare to dig the attack from the teacher. The teacher aims the ball between the players so they can practice moving to cover the ball; the goal is for the blocker to move inside for the ball while the defender moves behind. By moving in parallel lines, the players avoid colliding with each other. The blocker has the first chance to get to the ball. The defender has the second chance to dig the ball to the target. The blocker and defender return to their lines after each attempt. Four other players are designated as shaggers and a target. After three minutes, blockers move to the digging line, diggers assume the roles of shaggers and target, and the shaggers and target become blockers.

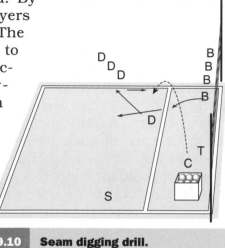

9.10 **Seam digging drill.**

BACK-ROW ATTACK EXCHANGE

In this drill, you practice defending against a back-row attack in a gamelike situation. Three diggers begin deep in the court on side A (figure 9.11). Three other diggers begin on side B. Six other diggers form three lines at the end of side B. Two players on either side of the net are designated setters. A teacher positioned near zone 5 on side B initiates the drill by tossing a ball to the setter. The setter sets to one of the back-row defenders, who attacks the ball deep into side A.

If the ball is not kept in play by the players on side A, all three defenders on side B run under the net to dig on side A. One of the side A defenders must retrieve the ball and place it in the basket. All three side A defenders run to the end of side B and get in one of the lines.

If the ball is kept in play, the rally continues until one team cannot return the ball over the net. If the defenders on side A win the rally, they remain in place for the next rally. One of the side B diggers must retrieve the ball and place it in the basket. All three side B diggers join one of the lines at the end of side B. Three new players step onto the court to begin the next rally. Different players should rotate into the setting position every two minutes.

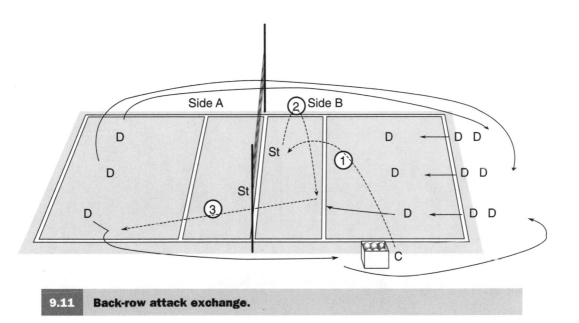

9.11 **Back-row attack exchange.**

DEFENSE VERSUS FREE BALL OFFENSE

In this drill, you will work on team defense against a free ball offense. Six players begin in base positions for team defense on one side of the net (figure 9.12). A teacher stands near the right sideline next to the defenders. On the opposite side of the court, six players begin in a W formation, with the player in court zone 2 ready to be the setter. Six other players work as ball shaggers, retrieving balls and placing them in the basket. The teacher tosses an easy free ball to the offensive players, who attack against the defense. The rally continues until one team does not return the ball across the net. After five tosses from the teacher, players on each side of the net rotate one position. The drill continues until each player has rotated to all zones of the court. After 30 plays, offensive players move under the net to become the defending team.

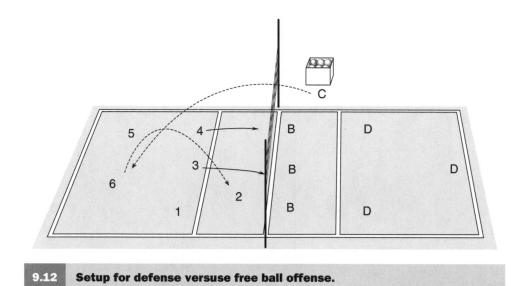

9.12 Setup for defense versuse free ball offense.

BONUS BALL

Let's focus on team defense in a fast-moving, competitive situation. Six players are assigned to each side of the court in specialized positions (figure 9.13). Each team begins the rally in transition positions. Four additional players around the court retrieve balls, and two feeders stand near one of the sidelines with a basket of balls nearby. Each feeder begins with three white volleyballs and one multicolor ball. The feeder tosses the ball to the team on the opposite side of the net throughout the drill. The first ball is tossed to side A. The winner of the rally gets the next ball. The first team to win three rallies (three white volleyballs) gets a multicolor ball tossed to them. This bonus ball is the only chance to win in this drill. The team receiving the bonus ball wins one point if they win the rally. If the opponent wins the rally, the drill continues until the opponent has won a total of three rallies and receives the bonus ball. This represents that team's opportunity to win a point. After a team has won three points, the front- and back-row players switch positions but remain in their specialized court zones. The first team to win six points wins the drill. The shaggers and feeders rotate onto the court to play, with one team rotating off to work as shaggers and feeders.

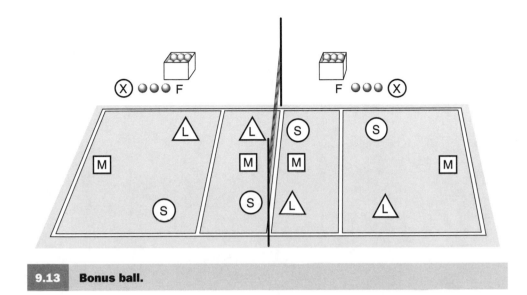

9.13 Bonus ball.

CHAPTER

Team Offense

In chapter 1, you learned a basic offensive system, the W formation. In the W formation, whoever is in court zone 2 is the setter, and players in court zones 3 and 4 are the primary attackers. One benefit of this system is that all six players gain experience in each court position.

Participants introduced to most sport activities typically find that they have natural strengths and weaknesses among the different skills associated with a particular sport. This is true for volleyball as well. In this chapter, we will build on the specialization concepts introduced in chapter 9, applying them to offense.

Modified 4-2

Let's keep the player designations from chapter 9 (see page 84). We can continue to use the W as the foundation of our offensive system, but let's add some rules. Players 7 and 10 (circles) are the setters/right-side players. Our initial offensive system requires them to be setters whenever they are in the front row. This means that when the opponent serves, they need to move to the target (court zone 2, net zone 6). The remaining players must prepare for the serve by getting in the ready position in a W formation.

Since two players are designated setters, the other four players can be designated attackers when in the front row. The two front-row attackers must be prepared to attack in court zones 3 and 4 once the ball is passed. Once the serve is returned across the net, players must switch to their specialized positions.

This offensive system is referred to as an international or modified 4-2 (figure 10.1). The 4 represents the number of players designated as attackers when in the front row. The 2 represents the number of players designated as setters when in the front row.

You might wonder why this offense is called a modified 4-2. Many people have been exposed to some form of volleyball where the setter is the player in court zone 3 (middle front). When two players are designated setters in the front row, and they perform their setting duties in court zone 3, this is referred to as a 4-2. The simple modification to this once-popular system is to have the setter in court zone 2. This allows both front-row attack options to be front sets.

Switching on offense is more complicated than switching on defense since you can't switch until your team puts the ball across the net. Let's examine the first rotation in a modified 4-2. At the moment of service, the designated setter, player 10, moves across the court to the target (figure 10.1b). Player 11 receives the serve, passing the ball to player 10. The attackers, players 8 and 9, move into position to attack the set from player 10. Player 10 sets the ball to player 9, who attacks it and sends it over the net (figure 10.1c). Once the ball crosses the net, the players move into their defensive or transition positions (figure 10.1d), preparing to defend the attack from the opponent.

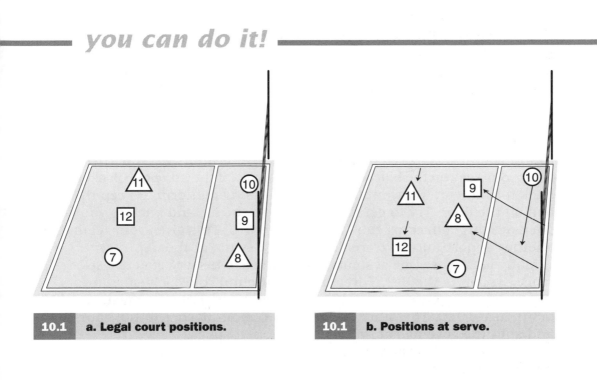

10.1 a. Legal court positions.

10.1 b. Positions at serve.

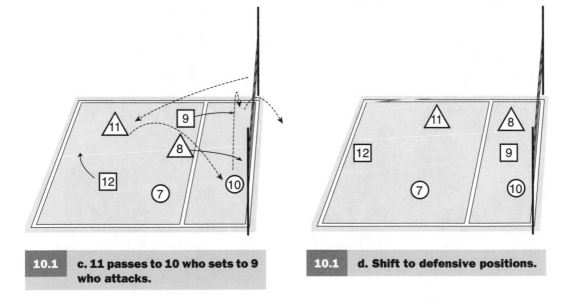

10.1 c. 11 passes to 10 who sets to 9 who attacks.

10.1 d. Shift to defensive positions.

Covering the Blocked Ball   We know what the defense is going to try to do against our attack. They want to put a wall of hands in front of our attacker and finish the play with a roof (see chapter 7). Our offense can protect our court against a blocked ball by having the five nonattacking players take part in covering the court.

Individual and team coverage can take away the potential momentum of a great block. To cover, move in a low position to surround the attacker. Keep your arms low and apart as you cover. Keep your eyes on the blocker's hands. Usually, if the attack is blocked back to you, you will want to use your passing platform to keep the ball off the floor. Try to get the ball high in the air and back to your offensive target in court zone 2 and net zone 6. This gives your team another opportunity in transition to get a swing at the net.

Many team coverage systems can be used. One very effective coverage system is the 3-2. Three players attempt to closely surround the attacker to prevent a blocked ball from hitting the floor near the net (figure 10.2). The other two players remain deeper in the court and split the coverage of the remaining open space.

Having added this additional component of the game, we can now put it all together with our team offense.

10.2   Surround the attacker.

Transition to Coverage   Let's look at the transition to coverage in rotation 1 (figure 10.3). As the attacker is getting ready to send the ball across the net, the other players move to coverage positions (the 3-2). Once the ball crosses the net, they switch to specialized positions. Player 11 receives the serve, passing it to player 10, who sets it as player 9 runs for the attack (figure 10.3b). Players 11, 10, and 8 surround the attacker (3-2 coverage system for left-side attack; figure 10.3c). After the attack crosses the net, players transition from coverage to base defense (figure 10.3d).

Transition to the 3-2

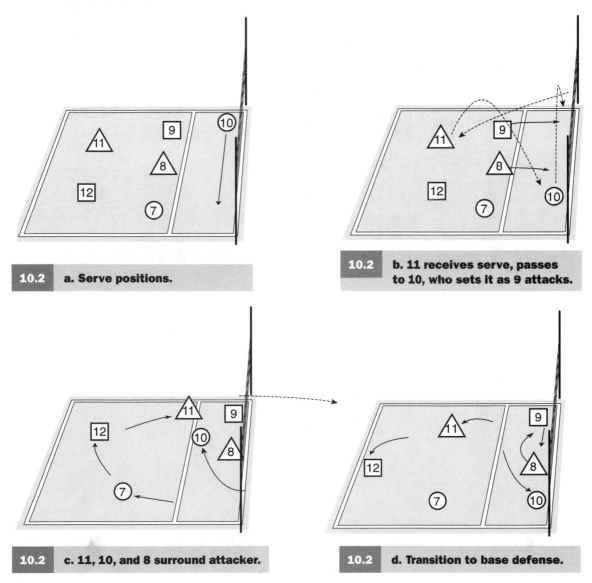

10.2	a. Serve positions.

10.2	b. 11 receives serve, passes to 10, who sets it as 9 attacks.

10.2	c. 11, 10, and 8 surround attacker.

10.2	d. Transition to base defense.

The 6-2 Offense By this time, you may be wondering why we introduced the back set. Our next offensive system description will provide the answer. Let's make one small change in our modified 4-2 offense. Using the same players, we will designate our two setters for the job of setting when they are in the back row. That means the setters join the other four players as attackers when in the front row. We now have six players designated as attackers when in the front row, and two of those players have the additional job of setting when in the back row. This offense is called a 6-2 (figure 10.4).

6-2 Offense

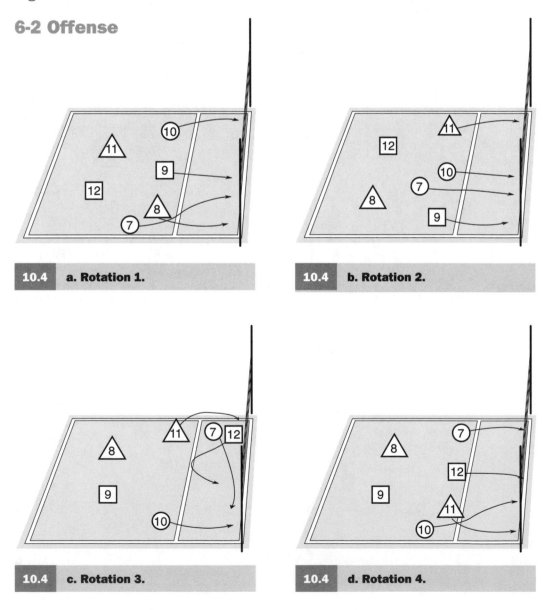

10.4 a. Rotation 1.

10.4 b. Rotation 2.

10.4 c. Rotation 3.

10.4 d. Rotation 4.

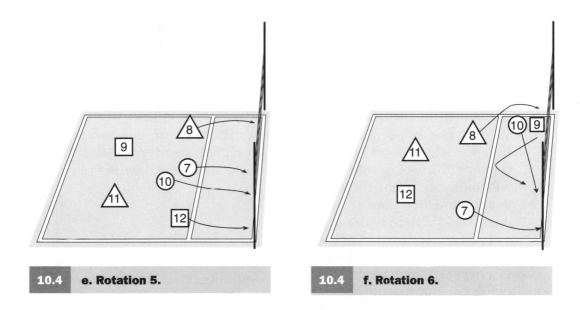

| 10.4 | e. Rotation 5. |

| 10.4 | f. Rotation 6. |

The setter still goes to the same target at the net, but now the right-side attacker can be a back set option in addition to our two front set options.

The keys to running a 6-2 revolve around the initial court position and movement of the designated setter. The back-row setter needs to be as close to the target as possible at the moment of serve and should be prepared for the constant transitions on the court between zones 1 and 2. We will take a closer look at the transition movements of the setter in chapter 11.

Since the setter in a 6-2 is legally in the back row, we need to establish the serve reception positions for each rotation to avoid overlap violations. In the first rotation, the team is still in a W formation, and the setter (player 7) hides behind player 8. At the moment of service, the setter runs to the target before the serve crosses the net and prepares to run the offense. Following our specialization rule, the setter in a 6-2 must return to a back-row base position once the ball crosses the net to the opponent.

The 5-1 Offense What if a team decides to use one setter all the time? All we need to do is designate player 7 to set all the time. Player 10 will no longer be a setter, but just an attacker in the front row. This would create a 5-1 offense—an offense in which five players attack when they are in the front row and one player sets all the time. Essentially, a 5-1 occurs when we use a 6-2 half the time and a modified 4-2 half the time. In a 5-1 offense, the player in the rotation opposite the setter is referred to as the *opposite.*

Offensive Passing

One benefit of specialization is that it allows a team to play the percentages. Allowing your best setters to set the ball or your tallest players to block in the middle increases your chances of success. This is true for serve reception as well. The W formation is a foundation for a passing system that has every nonsetter sharing in the responsibility of passing. If you watch accomplished teams play, you will likely see that they use fewer than five players. You may ask, "Where is the W?"

Teams can easily require their most effective passers to cover a larger part of the court by eliminating the responsibility of passing from one or more players. You may have noticed that the passer right in the middle of the W sometimes seems to get in the way. By making a simple adjustment in any of our rotations, we can use a four-passer system. Let's look at an example.

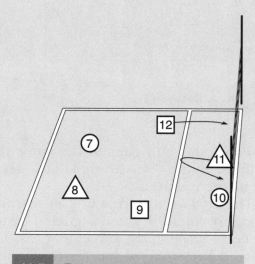

10.5 Four-passer system.

The player in court zone 3 (player 11) hides at the net. At the moment of serve, player 11 runs to the attack line to prepare to attack. Now we are using a four-passer system (figure 10.5).

If player 9 is the next-weakest passer, we could hide player 9 along the endline, removing any passing responsibility from that player. Keeping player 11 at the net and player 9 along the endline would result in a three-passer system (figure 10.6).

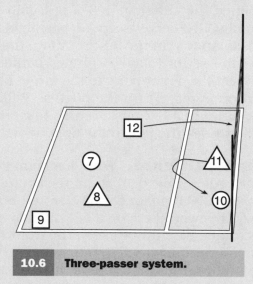

10.6 Three-passer system.

Finally, we could keep player 12 near the net and rely on two players to cover the whole court in a two-passer system (figure 10.7).

There are many passing system options. The critical aspect is that players are placed on the court legally, avoiding overlap violations. Even if you use a passing system with fewer than five players, keep in mind that the W still provides a comfortable and effective formation for handling every free

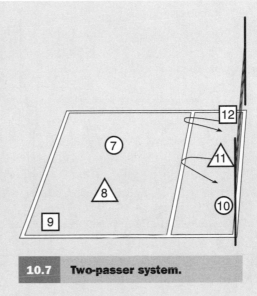

10.7 **Two-passer system.**

ball that your opponent gives you during a rally. It would not be at all unusual for a team to use a passing system with three designated passers in each rotation but continue to use the W for every free ball during transition.

Give it a go: Offense

COVERAGE DRILL

In the coverage drill (figure 10.8), you will practice moving to coverage positions by surrounding an attacker. Six players form an attacking line near court zone 4. All attackers except the first player in line has a volleyball. One player is the designated setter. Two blockers begin on the opposite side of the net near court zone 2. The second attacker in line tosses the ball to the setter. The setter sets a 14 to the first attacker in line. The setter and tosser move into coverage positions and play the ball if it is blocked back into their court. The attacker retrieves the ball at the end of the play and returns to the end of the attacking line. Every three minutes, three attackers move into the setting and blocking roles.

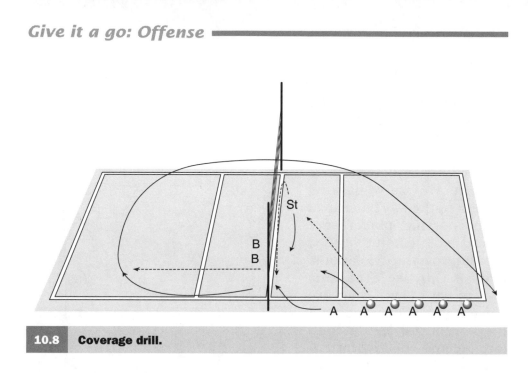

10.8 Coverage drill.

FIVE IN EACH ROTATION

Six players prepare to receive serve in rotation 1 of an international 4-2 offense (figure 10.9). Three blockers and three defenders are on the opposite side of the net. Six additional players serve as ball collectors. One of the defenders begins the drill by serving. The offensive team receives five consecutive serves, then moves to rotation 2. After the offensive team has taken five serves in each rotation, the ball collectors form the offensive team. The offense moves across the net to play defense, and the defensive players collect balls as the drill continues. Repeat until each group of six players has been on offense, defense, and assigned to collect balls.

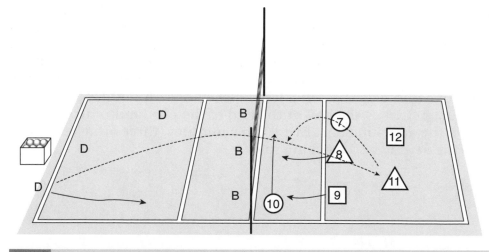

10.9 Five in each rotation drill.

Transition

Imagine a backyard volleyball scene. What is missing from most recreational games? It's *transition*. Transition needs to be a big part of your focus in learning how to play. If you watch accomplished players in a six-on-six competition, you will notice that the front-row players are either at the net or away from the net; rarely do they stand three to five feet away from the net.

We have established offensive systems that place players in positions to be able to receive the serve and then attack from the attack line or the back row. We have established base positions for each defender and a few defensive systems. Now we need to consider the movement required for players to transition from defense to offense and from offense to defense.

From Defense to Offense

The first priority for transition from defense to offense is the free ball, since this is the most common situation a team will face during play.

As your opponent attempts to gain ball control with their first and second touch, all defenders need to anticipate the likelihood of the third touch being an attack. If the first and second touch are not controlled effectively, you will likely receive a free ball. All defenders must quickly call "free" the moment they sense your opponent will not jump and swing on a second touch in the air.

As the defenders call "free," they need to begin moving to the W. Depending on the offensive system being used, the designated setter releases from base defensive position immediately upon hearing the "free" call and runs to the target.

The transition movement drill (page 107) allows two teams to practice this movement of alternating from defense to a W. Communication is the key. A chorus of voices shouting "free" should always coincide with the movement of all six players to their offensive formation. Ideally, the transition for a free ball should be completed before the ball crosses the net.

The individual movement of players in this free ball transition is critical. Front-row blockers are positioned at the net on defense (figure 11.1a). The free ball signal requires all front-row designated attackers to retreat to the attack line (figure 11.1b). Often players will backpedal, using many small steps to arrive near the attack line. This type of movement is inefficient.

Volleyball requires running. Players need to cover 5- or 10-foot spaces quickly. Front-row players begin to transition on a free ball by turning from the net, keeping their eyes on the opponent's court, and (taking a long running step) toward the attack line, followed by two quick smaller steps. In most cases, three running steps are all that is needed.

Back-row defenders, especially players in court zones 1 and 5, use a similar footwork pattern to move from their defensive base to the area of the court they are responsible for defending.

Each player must also move quickly from offense to defense. Typically, this requires moving from team coverage position to base defensive position. Remember to move quickly and keep your eyes on the ball in the opponent's court throughout this transition. Long rallies produce multiple opportunities for players to transition from defense to offense, attempting to counterattack or control a free ball.

11.1 a. Basic defensive positions.

11.1 b. Move into offensive positions.

The Setter   Transition for the back-row setter is a challenge. On defense, this player expects to dig the ball. At the same time, the setter needs to read and react quickly to every attack that is directed at a teammate. In this situation, the setter needs to release quickly to the target and prepare to move to the ball that is successfully dug and run a transition offense. The numbering system for set height and location is extremely important in transition because the attackers need to signal the setter verbally while the ball is in the air. The setter often hears more than one player calling for a set. Although this can be confusing, it is also helpful for the setter to know who is ready to attack.

One of the great benefits of specialization is that we have two potential setters on the right side of the court. Since the setter needs to play defense at the moment of each attack, the designated setter in any offensive system is likely to be the player to dig the ball at times. A setter who is also a back-row defender needs to dig the ball to the target area, allowing the right-side player in the front row (referred to as the secondary setter) to set the ball in transition.

The designated setter in the front row may also be in a position to dig a ball, especially as an off-blocker. In this case, the setter should dig the ball high into the middle of the court so that the right-side player in zone 1 can move in to set the ball in transition. The setter digging drill (page 108) is effective in training right-side players to work together in transition from digging to setting.

Down Ball Opportunities   A free ball opportunity occurs when an opposing player prepares to use a passing platform or hands to direct a third team contact over the net. A defensive team might also respond to a player executing a down ball (attack from the floor) on the third team contact with a free ball signal.

Blocking a down ball is not a high-percentage play. In fact, an attacker who did not jump to attack would find blocking hands above the net a very inviting target. As players gain experience, they should be encouraged to react to a down ball as a free ball.

Transition Between Skills

Players also need to work on transition movements between skills. Some drills combine two or more skills. These combination drills are often more gamelike and simulate competitive situations while allowing repetition for skill development. A drill designed for players to serve and then immediately dig a ball would be an example of a drill combining two consecutive touches by a player. Combination drills can also be developed to utilize a series of several movements and touches. Let's try some of these drills.

Give it a go: Transition

TRANSITION MOVEMENT

The transition movement drill (figure 11.2) makes you practice moving from defense to the W formation on a free ball and back to base defensive positions. Six players on side A begin in specialized base defensive positions. Six players on side B begin in specialized free ball court positions for an international 4-2 offense. The teacher or coach signals "free ball," and the team on side A immediately moves to a free ball court formation while the team on side B moves to base defensive positions. The teacher signals "free ball" again, and the teams quickly move back to their original court positions. The teacher signals "free ball" four more times and players transition. Front- and back-row players switch positions on each team and repeat the drill.

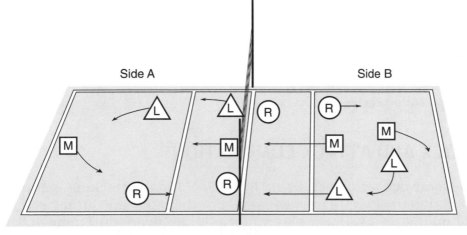

| **11.2** | **Transition movement drill.** |

SETTER DIGGING

The setters practice working together to dig an attack that can be set by a teammate. Two players begin in base defensive position in court zones 1 and 2 (figure 11.3). Four attackers form a line near zone 4. A teacher is positioned on a box in court zone 2. Six players work together as collectors and feeders. The teacher initiates the drill by tossing the ball in the air, simulating a set. Defenders transition to defensive positions. The back-row defender attempts to dig the ball to the target as the front-row setter moves to the ball and sets a 14. The front-row defender attempts to dig the ball high into the middle of the court to allow the back-row defender to move and set a 14. In either situation, the outside hitter attacks the ball, retrieves the attack, and returns to the end of the attack line. The two defenders quickly move back to their base defensive positions. The drill is repeated for 10 attempts. The setters then switch front- and back-row base positions and run through 10 more attempts. The setters and attackers switch roles with the other six players.

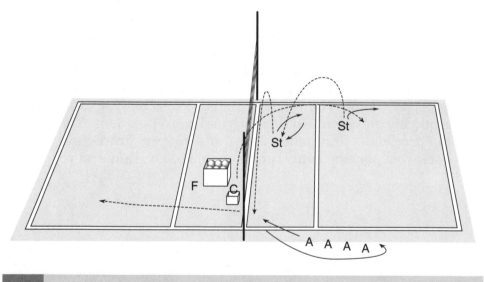

11.3   **Setter digging drill.**

BLOCK AND ATTACK COMBINATION

The footwork for transitioning from blocking to attacking is fundamental to the execution of the skill. For the block and attack combination (figure 11.4), six players form a line near court zone 4. The first player gets into a ready blocking position. A teacher is positioned near zone 2 and signals "block" to begin the drill. The blocker executes a block and runs to the attack line as the teacher prepares to toss the ball to simulate a 14 set. The blocker approaches and attacks the ball, runs to retrieve it, and places it in the basket before returning to the end of the line. The drill continues until each player has had 10 attempts.

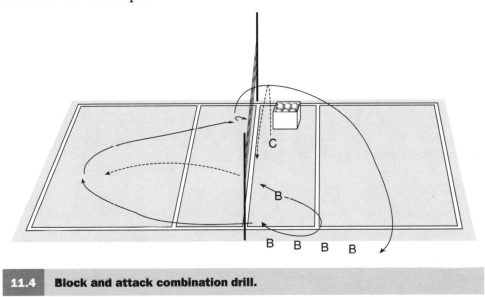

11.4 **Block and attack combination drill.**

LEFT VERSUS LEFT

Now let's practice team transition while working on all skills, with emphasis on left-side attacking. Two teams of six players are on each side of the court in specialized court positions (figure 11.5). Tossers stand close to the sidelines near court zone 5 on each side of the net. Four players collect volleyballs. The tosser on side A initiates the drill by tossing a volleyball high in the air to the target on side A. The designated setter on side A moves to play the ball. Setters must set to the left-side attacker on each toss but can set to any other player during rallies. The drill continues until one team cannot return the ball over the net. The team that wins each rally gets the next toss. Every play results in a point, and the game is played until one team reaches 15 points. The tossers and ball collectors switch roles with one of the teams at the end of each game.

You can modify this drill to work on right-side attacking and middle attacking. For right-side attacking, follow all the rules for the left versus left drill, except that each ball from the tosser must be set to the right-side attacker. For middle attacking, follow all the rules for the left versus left drill, except that each ball from the tosser must be set to the middle attacker.

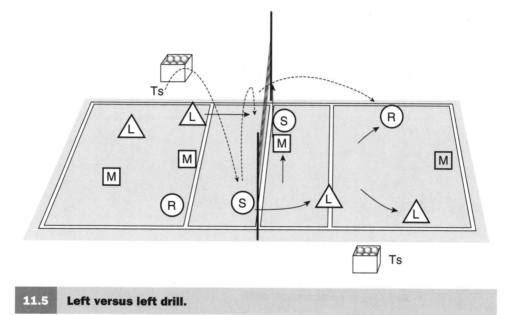

11.5 **Left versus left drill.**

12

CHAPTER

Modified Games

To enhance the learning process, the game of volleyball and many of the drills presented could easily be modified based on the number of participants, courts, or volleyballs. Modifying game rules is a way of increasing the focus on one specific skill. Rules could be relaxed to allow unlimited contacts in the interest of keeping the ball in play. Practice opportunities can be enhanced by using volleyballs of different sizes and weights. Creating smaller courts puts greater emphasis on ball control, whereas limiting the number of players on the court can force players to cover more court space and get them more repetitions.

Doubles Anyone?

Doubles is probably the most common modification. Let's look at a typical doubles offense.

To cover a regulation-size court, a doubles team splits the court. One player begins near court zone 1 and the other player near court zone 5. Servers often try to serve to court zone 6, since this will split the two players. Passers need to anticipate the direction of the serve quickly, with one player clearly signaling "mine" while the other player releases and moves to the middle of the court near the attack line. This area of the court is the target area for the passer in doubles. The player receiving serve sends the ball to the target area, then moves toward the net to attack.

Once a doubles team mounts an attack, they need to transition to defensive positions. If the level of play results in a strong attack from an opponent, then one defender should remain at the net to block, leaving the other player to cover the rest of the court. The blocker should indicate whether she will attempt to block the line or crosscourt area, so that the defender can move to cover the exposed area of the court. At the moment of service, blockers can use hand signals, with one finger indicating a line block (figure 12.1a) and two fingers indicating a crosscourt block (figure 12.1b)

If the level of play does not result in strong attacks, both players should share responsibility for half of the court on defense (figure 12.1c).

If a smaller court is used, players can play in a tandem formation, with one player at the net ready to set and one player covering all of the space as a passer (figure 12.1d). Once the team goes on defense, the setter stays at the net to block and the passer covers the rest of the space as a digger.

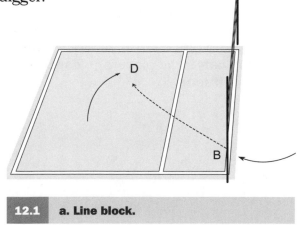

| 12.1 | a. Line block. |

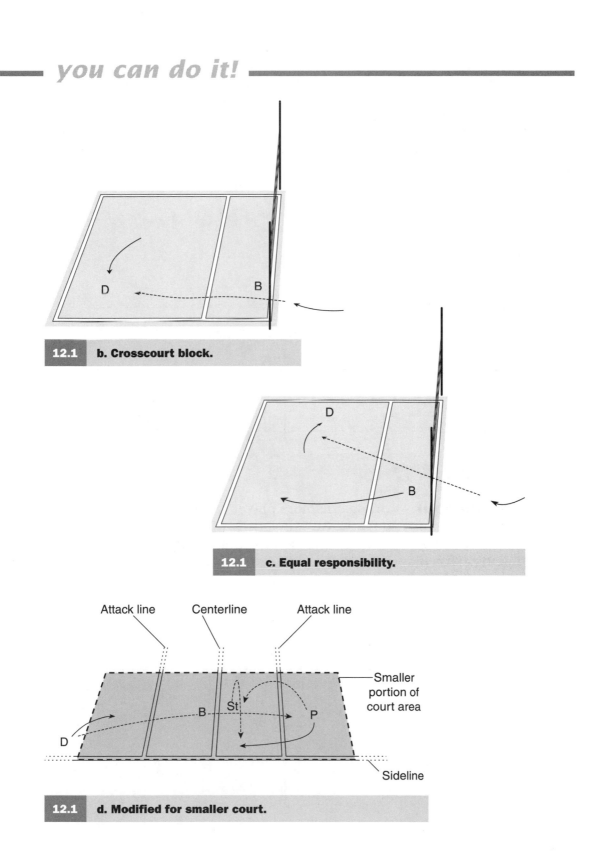

12.1   **b. Crosscourt block.**

12.1   **c. Equal responsibility.**

Attack line   Centerline   Attack line

Smaller portion of court area

Sideline

12.1   **d. Modified for smaller court.**

Now that we have taken a look at the doubles game, let's go over the court positions and responsibilities in games organized for fewer than six players.

Three on Three   In triples, a team uses a modified doubles format and adds a designated net player to serve as the primary setter and blocker on each play. This results in a triangle formation (figure 12.2). The other two players can serve primarily as passers, diggers, and attackers.

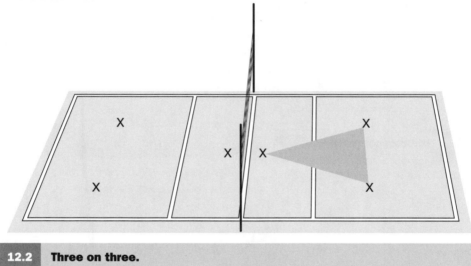

| 12.2 | **Three on three.** |

Four on Four   Adding one more player to the court creates a diamond formation (figure 12.3). The fourth player moves to the deep part of the court and has primary responsibility for passing and digging. This player could also attack from the back row.

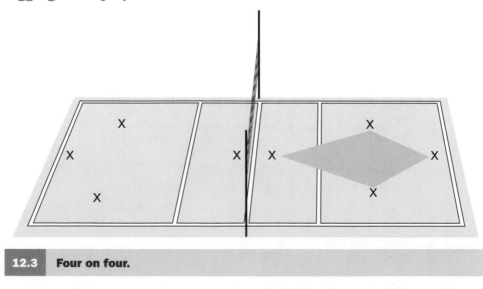

| 12.3 | **Four on four.** |

Five on Five When playing with five players, it's best to go back to the offensive formations discussed in chapter 10 and simply play without the right back player (figure 12.4). This adaptation minimizes the changes necessary to play, since you still have three front-row players. Using an international 4-2 style of play, simply require the two back-row players to cover a little more court space than they would in a six-on-six game.

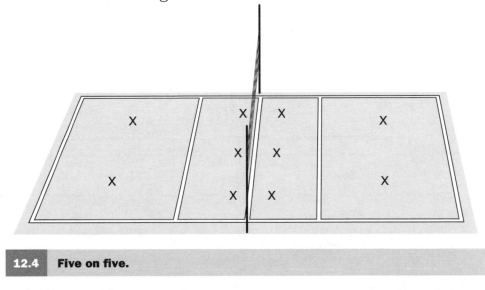

12.4 Five on five.

ONE-ON-ONE PASSING

Work with a partner to pass the ball back and forth over the net (figure 12.5). Attempt to get the ball over the net 10 times in a row without an error. This repetition will help you work out any flaws in your passing technique.

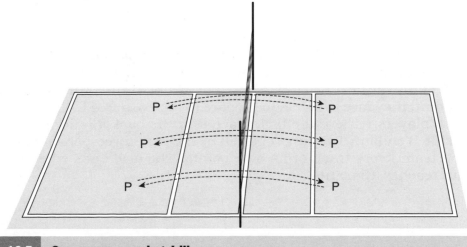

12.5 One-on-one passing drill.

TWO-ON-TWO SETTING

Divide the court in half lengthwise and form four teams of two players (figure 12.6). Each team works together within a quarter of the court. As the ball crosses the net, a player calls for the ball as his teammate releases and moves toward the attack area. The receiver sets the ball to his teammate, who sets the ball over the net beyond the opponent's attack line. The teams set the ball back and forth until someone makes an error.

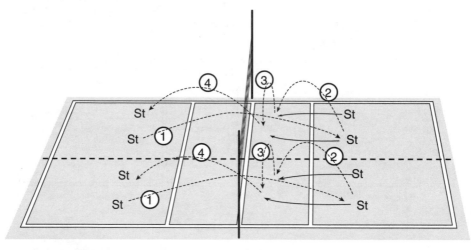

| 12.6 | Two-on-two setting drill. |

TRIPLES

To get you used to using three contacts consistently, try the triples drill (figure 12.7). Groups of three players set up in a triangle formation on both side A and side B. Two groups of three players stand on the endline of side B. A teacher located near zone 5 on side B tosses a free ball to side A to initiate each rally. If side A wins the rally and a point, they stay on the court, and the side B players retrieve the ball, place it in the basket, and move to the side B endline. They are replaced by the next three-person team. If side B wins the rally and the point, they race to side A to prepare to receive a free ball, and the side A players retrieve the ball, place it in the basket, and move to the side B endline. They are replaced by the next three-person team. Each team keeps track of its own points. The drill ends when one team reaches 15 points.

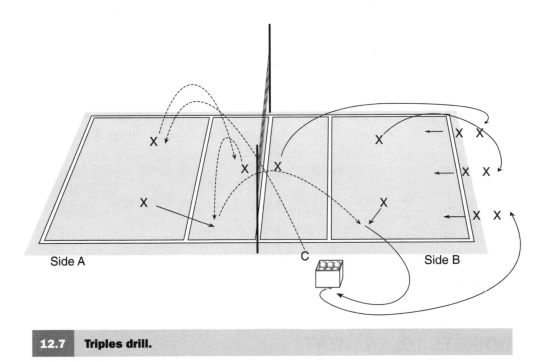

12.7 **Triples drill.**

QUEEN/KING OF THE COURT

This drill uses the concept of three-on-three volleyball. Teams of three players begin on both side A and side B (figure 12.8). Two additional teams stand on the endline of side B. A server on side B initiates the rally. If side A wins the rally, they get a point and remain in position. Side B retrieves the ball and returns to the endline. The next team of three steps onto side B. If side B wins the rally, they get a point and move to side A. The next team of three steps onto side B and initiates the next rally with a serve. Side A retrieves the ball and returns to the endline. Each team keeps track of its own points. The drill ends when one of the teams reaches 15 points.

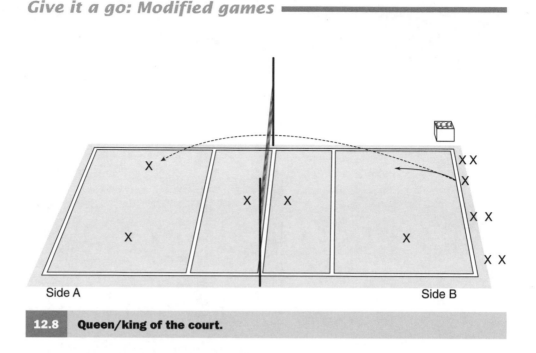

Side A   Side B

| 12.8 | **Queen/king of the court.** |

DOUBLES TOURNAMENT

It's time for a competitive two-on-two tournament. If possible, use three courts (figure 12.9). This allows six teams (12 players) to compete at the same time—two teams on each court with any additional teams at the endline of each court getting ready to play. You can modify this drill based on the number of courts and participants. Each game is played to seven points using rally scoring (a point scored on each play regardless of who is serving).

On court one, players are required to comply with only two rules: no net violations and the serve must initiate from the endline. On court two, a rule is added—a minimum of two team contacts must be used by each team every time the ball crosses the net. On court three, three team contacts are required each time the ball crosses the net. On courts two and three, a block does not count as a team contact for the blocking team; however, an attacking team that has a ball returned from a block must restart their count for team contacts.

There is an exception to the two- and three-contact rules. One team contact is allowed on any court if a player can jump and attack the team's first team contact from a ball that crosses near the net.

Players on each team keep track of the number of games they win. Teams that win a game move to the end of the line on the next court, moving to the right. A team that wins on court three moves to the endline of court three or stays on the court if only one team is waiting on the endline. Teams that lose a game move to the endline of the next court to their left. A team that loses on court one moves to the endline of court one. The tournament continues for a designated time period. Each team reports its total wins at the end of the tournament.

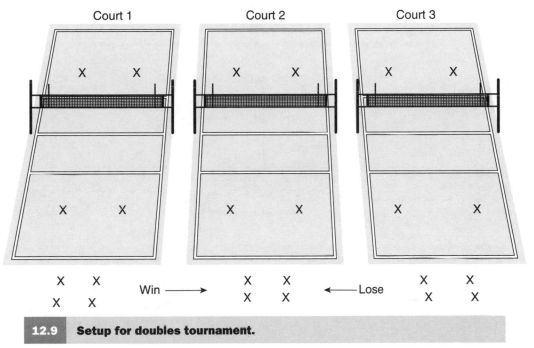

12.9 **Setup for doubles tournament.**

REVERSE COED DOUBLES

Play using a women's-height net. Coed teams of two are formed on each available court (figure 12.10). Reverse coed rules allow women to attack at the net. Men are allowed to attack only from behind the attack line. Two teams begin on the court with a tosser stationed next to the sideline near zone 5 on side B. Another coed team helps retrieve volleyballs. The team on side A receives six tosses in a row. The tosser alternates tossing to the male and female player on the team. The receiving team follows reverse coed rules on each play and uses three contacts to return the ball to side B. The side B players follow reverse coed rules throughout the rally. At the end of each rally, a ball is tossed to the side A team. After six attempts, the side A players become retrievers, the side B players move to side A, and the retrievers move to side B.

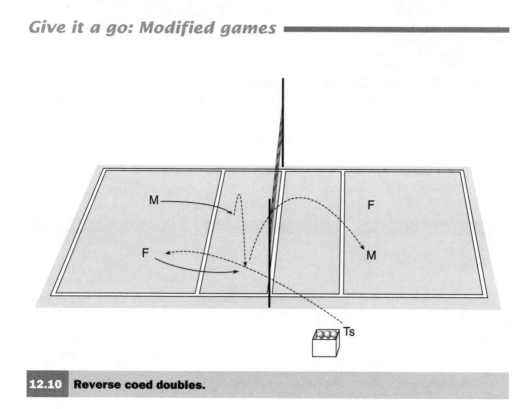

12.10 Reverse coed doubles.

CHAPTER

Scoring Systems

For many years, traditional scoring in volleyball meant that only the serving team could score points. The first team to earn 15 points won the game, although they needed to win by 2 points. Winning a match required winning a series of games, usually a best-of-three series.

The sport of volleyball has changed considerably just in the past few decades. At many levels, best-of-three matches have been replaced with best-of-five matches. Scoring has changed as well.

The scoring changes have been as significant as any of the new rules. Many, if not most, of the rule changes have been driven by international volleyball issues related to marketing the sport, for example, making the game more user-friendly to the television industry. Under the old rules, live television coverage of a match could require anywhere from an hour to two and a half hours.

Timed games have been used, most often with the outdoor beach game. Timing the game is an effective way to establish a definitive starting and ending point for a match.

In some cases, the idea of capping a game has been used. A capped game allows a team to win by a one-point margin.

Bonus scoring has also been tried. Bonus scoring uses traditional scoring, except the serving team scores two points when they serve and win a rally. The nonserving team scores one point if they win the rally.

Rally scoring was first introduced as a way to decide a close match. The deciding game of a match would move from traditional scoring to rally scoring, in which a point was scored on every play, regardless of who served.

Recent changes have adopted the rally format for all games and extended the total points needed for victory to 25 or 30 points, depending on the level of play. One thing is clear—when people come together to play, they have to agree on the rules before they start competing.

The wide variety of scoring systems will help you participate in drills and games that will be exciting and keep your attention. The traditional scoring method, in which a game goes to 15 points, can become discouraging if your team is on the wrong end of a 2-13 score.

Using Cones

Momentum describes the apparent shifts in control from one team to another. Let's look at a fun way to see the momentum changes as they occur during a game. Decide for yourself if momentum is real or not.

We will use the transition movement drill from chapter 11 (page 107), but we will add a server to initiate play. Teams move from defense to offense to defense throughout the drill. Notice the large cones that have been added on the sideline (figure 13.1). This is the visible scoreboard.

The drill begins with five large cones off the court and between the two attack lines. At the end of each rally, the winning team moves a large cone to their side of the court. The cone moves back to the middle when a team loses a rally. A team must get all five cones to their side to win the game. If a team wins four cones, then loses the next six plays, this way of scoring shows what loss of momentum looks like (figure 13.2). The other team, the one that was on the brink of losing, sees the tide turning as the cones start showing up on their side of the court.

13.1 Use cones to keep score.

13.2 The cones act as a visible scoreboard, clearly illustrating momentum shifts.

Using Points

Points are the most common way of scoring games and drills. Certain skills can be emphasized by awarding points for successful execution of a particular skill. For example, if you want to emphasize back-row attacking, you could play a game in which a point can be scored only when a team ends a rally with a back-row attack. Or you could use the bonus scoring idea and award three points to the team that successfully executes a back-row attack but only one point to the team that wins the rally any other way. This type of competition can get very exciting in a hurry; the team that is behind has the chance to catch up quickly by going for bonus points.

Competitive games and drills also can be timed. Establishing a time limit helps manage a class period effectively and allows some control for maximizing player participation.

Wave Rotation

During a game, players rotate in a clockwise direction. In a drill or scrimmage game, players can rotate in several ways. One effective method of rotating is wave rotation (figure 13.3).

Think of the endline on side B as the ocean and the endline on side A as the shore. The waves move from side B to side A. This is a fun way to rotate players. The triples drill (chapter 12, page 116) uses wave rotation.

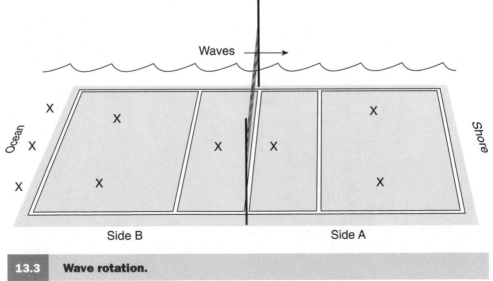

13.3 **Wave rotation.**

The Wash Method

One last scoring system that has gained incredible popularity is the wash method of scoring drills. For example, in a six-on-six game, each team serves once. If the same team wins both rallies, that team wins a point and gets to rotate. If the teams split the rallies, they wash each other out and the drill begins again. A team can win only when they have rotated six times, back to where they began. Instead of playing for points, each team plays for the chance to rotate. Instead of playing to 15 points, as in traditional scoring, each team essentially plays to 6 points.

This is an effective way for new learners to practice. If several rallies end up in a wash, players get to practice the same position for several rallies in a row. For example, a server who is struggling may get several chances to serve before either team wins a rotation. Furthermore, a team ahead on the scoreboard could easily get stuck in a rotation, and the opponent could get back in the game.

Wash scoring is also effective in a transition drill. Instead of serving each time, players could receive a free ball each time they win a rally. The bonus ball drill (chapter 9, page 90) is an example of a transition wash drill.

Handicap Scoring

If teams are unevenly matched, it is easy to handicap the scoring. For example, team A would serve twice and receive once, but needs to win all three rallies to rotate. Team B receives twice and serves once, but needs to win only two out of the three rallies to rotate.

Give it a go: Scoring

DIG, SET, ATTACK BONUS

Two teams of six play a game to 15 points. Side A serves first (figure 13.4). On each play, a team that scores from a dig, set, and attack gets three points and is awarded the next serve. (*Note:* A dig is defined as a reception from an attacker who jumped to attack either with a hard hit or an offspeed shot.)

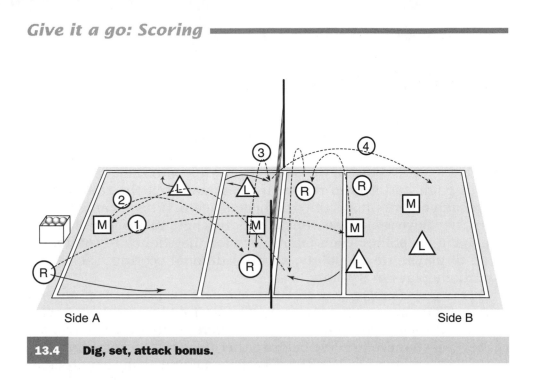

13.4   **Dig, set, attack bonus.**

FOUR-ON-FOUR WAVE

This is a four-on-four volleyball game that uses wave scoring. Two groups of four players begin on the court (figure 13.5). The team on side B serves to initiate the drill. At the end of the rally, the team on side A moves off the court and retrieves the ball. The team on side B moves to side A, and a new team steps onto side B and initiates the next rally with a serve.

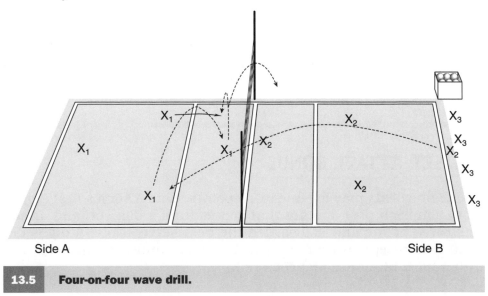

13.5   **Four-on-four wave drill.**

SIX-ON-SIX WASH

This is a good way to emphasize the importance of winning two rallies in a row. Two teams of six begin on the court (figure 13.6). The teams complete a two-play series. Side A serves first. Regardless of the outcome, side B serves next. If either team wins both plays, they earn the right to rotate. Another two-play series commences. If each team wins one of the plays in a series, it is considered a wash and the two-play series is repeated until a team earns the right to rotate. The first team to win six rotations wins the drill.

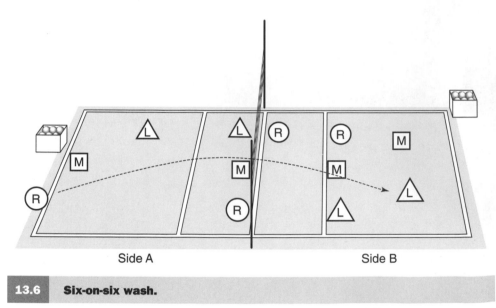

Side A   Side B

13.6   **Six-on-six wash.**

14

Off to the Endline

Volleyball can be a lifetime activity. Mastering the skills will take time, but you can do it. Just think about the progress you have made already. You are well equipped to take your game to another level. Remember that communication is the key. When players talk, they move. When they move, they are able to keep the ball off the floor and have a good opportunity to put it down on the opponent's court.

Pass, set, hit. Dig, set, hit. In many ways, that is what the game comes down to. Ball control is critical. Keep that in mind as you work on your game. Use two-person pepper drills (chapter 8, page 72) or three-person pepper drills to create lots of repetitions and contacts. Try to play modified games on a smaller court (see chapter 12). This will enable you to work on passing, setting, and attacking over the net.

Playing one-on-one volleyball (chapter 12) and allowing unlimited contacts for either player allows you to touch the ball often. You won't go wrong if you find lots of chances to play and are able to get as many touches as possible.

If the volleyball bug really bites you and you can't seem to get enough of the game, you will likely find yourself watching the highest levels of competitive play. You will see a lot of advanced tactics and specialization at work on the court.

At elite levels of play, players generally have well-defined roles and duties. Many players often compete only in the front or back row, enabling them to focus on their strengths and become well-skilled specialists.

Competitive teams can create exciting offensive plays by using the 1 through 9 numbering system and running a wide variety of plays with different combinations of play sets.

As you can imagine, there is a lot more to the game at the competitive level. Keep working on the fundamentals and you can soon look for opportunities to move to the next level.

Where can you play? The game is everywhere. Leagues are available through the YMCA and recreation department programs. Beach and grass court tournaments are organized according to ability level.

Walleyball is volleyball on a racquetball court. Walleyball provides all the thrills of volleyball with a few more angles to play.

Outdoor volleyball equipment is easy to purchase, set up, and store. It's a game for young and old. It's a game for you.

Substitutions

We haven't said much about substitutions. The rules of volleyball differ greatly from high school to the international game regarding the limits for substitutions. Perhaps the most important suggestion for instructional classes is to limit the maximum number of players on the court to six.

My introduction to volleyball during junior high school was the nine-per-side game. The rotation pattern was a zig-zag across the back row, then across the middle, and finally to the front row. Avoid this at all costs. If more than six players are on a team, simply place substitutes off the court near zones 4 and 2 (figure 14.1). Players rotate from zone 1 to zone 6 to

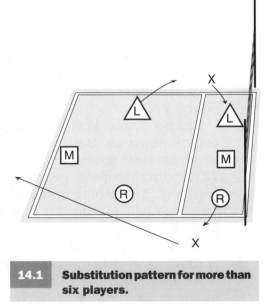

14.1 Substitution pattern for more than six players.

zone 5, then off the court for a play before returning to zone 4. Players then rotate from zone 4 to zone 3 to zone 2, and step off again for a play before going back to serve.

THREE-PERSON PEPPER

The three-person pepper drill (figure 14.2) is a good way to get dig, set, and attack repetitions. Groups of three players use available space on the courts. Players A and B stand at least 15 feet apart. Player C stands an equal distance from both players but slightly off to one side of the straight line formed by players A and B. Player A begins by hitting a down ball at player B. Player B digs the ball to player C, who sets it back to player B. Player B hits a down ball to player A, who digs the ball to player C. Player C sets the ball right back to player A. The sequence repeats for two minutes. After two minutes, all three players switch roles.

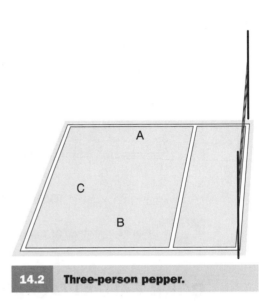

14.2 Three-person pepper.

ONE-ON-ONE VOLLEYBALL GAMES

One-on-one games (figure 14.3) are a good way to develop ball control. The first one-on-one game is played with the attack lines serving as the endlines. Players set the ball back and forth, scoring one point each time the ball hits the floor on their opponent's court or when the opponent cannot return the ball.

The second one-on-one game is modified to allow two consecutive contacts for each player and is played within the same modified court space. Play is initiated by a set over the net. The receiver passes to herself then sets the ball across the net. Points are awarded as in the first one-on-one game.

In the third one-on-one game, the court space extends back toward the endline of each side. The rules are modified to allow three contacts for each player. Each rally begins with a set across the net. The receiving player passes to herself, sets to herself, and attempts to jump and attack with the third contact. The game can be scored to 15 points or any predetermined number of points.

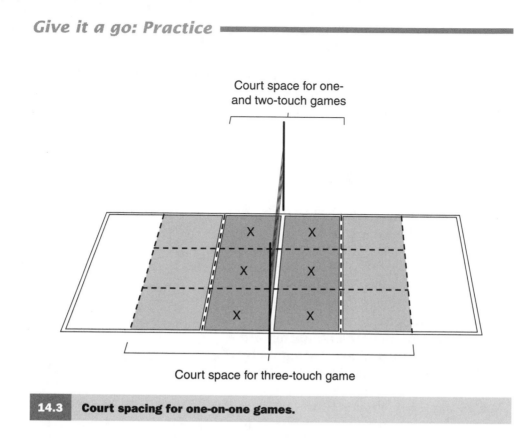

Court space for one-
and two-touch games

Court space for three-touch game

14.3 **Court spacing for one-on-one games.**

DOWN BALL ATTACKING

One group of six players forms a line near zone 4 (figure 14.4). The first player in line is at the net. Six other players collect balls and feed the teacher (who is located in zone 2) throughout the drill. The teacher begins the drill by tossing the ball high and near the attack line behind zone 4. The attacker at the net must quickly retreat and move behind the ball to execute a down ball attack. The attacker immediately goes to the end of the attacking line, and the next player in line moves to attack a down ball on the next toss from the teacher. The drill continues until each player has had eight down balls. Then the two groups switch roles.

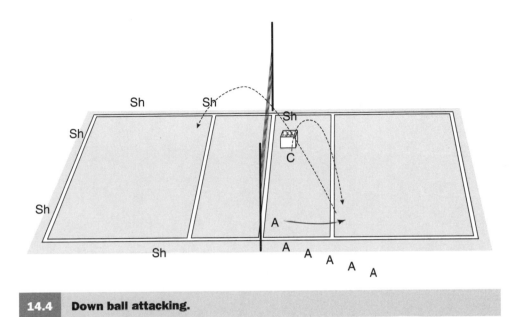

14.4 **Down ball attacking.**

Time to Play

Volleyball, like all sports, has its own etiquette and protocol. For example, competitive volleyball matches allow only the court captain and coach to communicate with the officials, and that communication is limited primarily to calling time-outs or requesting substitutions. Before a match begins, teams indicate they are ready for competition by lining up on the endline and waiting for the official's signal to enter the court and prepare for the first serve.

Now, go ahead, you're ready to head for the endline. Enjoy the game!

About the Writer

Joel Dearing is an associate professor of education and women's volleyball coach at Springfield College in Springfield, Massachusetts. During his 14-year coaching tenure at Springfield College, Dearing has established his program as one of the best in the nation. He has a 346-131 record at the school and ranks in the top 10 in Division III history with a 479-245 overall mark in 21 years as a women's coach.

Sports Fundamentals Series

Learning sports basics has never been more effective—or more fun—than with the new Sports Fundamentals Series. These books enable recreational athletes to engage in the activity quickly. Quick participation, not hours of reading, makes learning more fun and more effective.

Each chapter addresses a specific skill for that particular sport, leading the athlete through a simple, four-step sequence:

- *You Can Do It:* The skill is introduced with sequential instructions and accompanying photographs.
- *More to Choose and Use:* Variations and extensions of the primary skill are covered.
- *Take It to the Court/Field:* Readers learn how to apply the skill in competition.
- *Give It a Go:* These provide several direct experiences for gauging, developing, and honing the skill.

The writers of the Sports Fundamentals Series books are veteran instructors and coaches with extensive knowledge of their sport. They communicate clearly and succinctly, making reading and applying the content to the sport enjoyable for both younger and older recreational athletes. And with books on more and more sports being developed, you're sure to get up to speed quickly on any sport you want to play.

The Sports Fundamentals Series will include:

- Soccer
- Volleyball
- Weight Training
- Basketball
- Bowling
- Archery
- Golf
- Racquetball
- Softball
- Tennis

HUMAN KINETICS
The Premier Publisher for Sports & Fitness
P.O. Box 5076, Champaign, IL 61825-5076
www.HumanKinetics.com

To place your order, U.S. customers call
TOLL FREE 1-800-747-4457.
Customers outside the U.S. should place orders using the appropriate telephone number/address shown in the front of this book

The next step in skill development

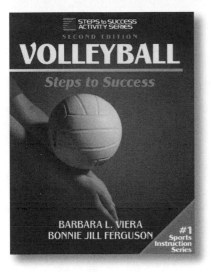

Volleyball: Steps to Success offers 12 easy-to-follow steps designed to help your players learn and practice key skills. The book features 99 drills that develop players' offensive and defensive skills. The drills come with performance goals and a list of key points to remember when executing each drill. Plus, many include instructions for increasing or decreasing the difficulty of the drill.

Each step is an easy transition from the one before. The first steps cover fundamental volleyball skills—correct posture, passing, and serving. As players progress, they will learn to execute more difficult techniques—attacks, blocks, and offensive and defensive systems.

ISBN 0-87322-646-1 • 1996 • 168 pages

Volleyball Drills for Champions provides 73 practice activities to produce the maximum individual player and team development.

Seven of the world's top volleyball coaches combined their knowledge to produce this special practice tool. Each coach focuses on one of volleyball's key skills:

- **Serving:** Russ Rose, Pennsylvania State University
- **Passing:** Lisa Love, University of Southern California
- **Setting:** John Dunning, University of the Pacific
- **Attacking:** Brad Saindon, Australia National Team
- **Blocking:** Greg Giovanazzi, University of Michigan
- **Digging:** Jim Stone, Ohio State University

In addition, editor Mary Wise, head coach at the University of Florida, contributes valuable insights for designing drills and incorporating them into effective practice sessions.

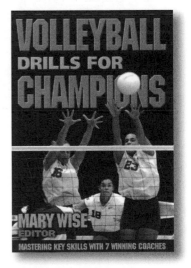

ISBN 0-88011-778-8 • 1999 • 192 pages

HUMAN KINETICS
The Premier Publisher for Sports & Fitness
P.O. Box 5076, Champaign, IL 61825-5076
www.HumanKinetics.com

To place your order, U.S. customers call
TOLL FREE 1-800-747-4457.
Customers outside the U.S. should place orders using the appropriate telephone number/address shown in the front of this book